PENTAX SFX

and SFX_N

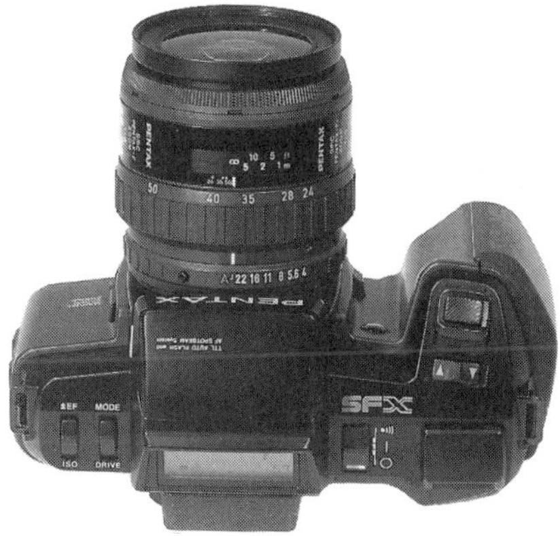

Richard Hünecke

HOVE ~ FOUNTAIN BOOKS

In U.S.A. and Canada

the Pentax SFX_N is known as the

PENTAX $SF1_N$

All text, illustrations and data apply to cameras with either name

U.S. Edition ISBN 0-906447-56-9

Pentax SFX

First English Edition February 1988
Second English Edition August 1989
Series Editor: Dennis Laney
Technical Editor: George Wakefield
Editor: Georgina Fuller
English Translation: Liselotte Sperl
Typeset by Oliver Dawkins Ltd, Burgess Hill
and Brighton Typesetting, Sussex
Printed in West-Germany by Schwabenverlag AG

ISBN 0-86343-220-4

Published by
HOVE FOUNTAIN BOOKS
the joint imprint of

Fountain Press Ltd
45 The Broadway, Tolworth
Surrey KT6 7DW

&

Hove Foto Books
34 Church Road, Hove
Sussex BN3 2GJ

U.K. Trade Distribution by
Fountain Press Ltd

Contents

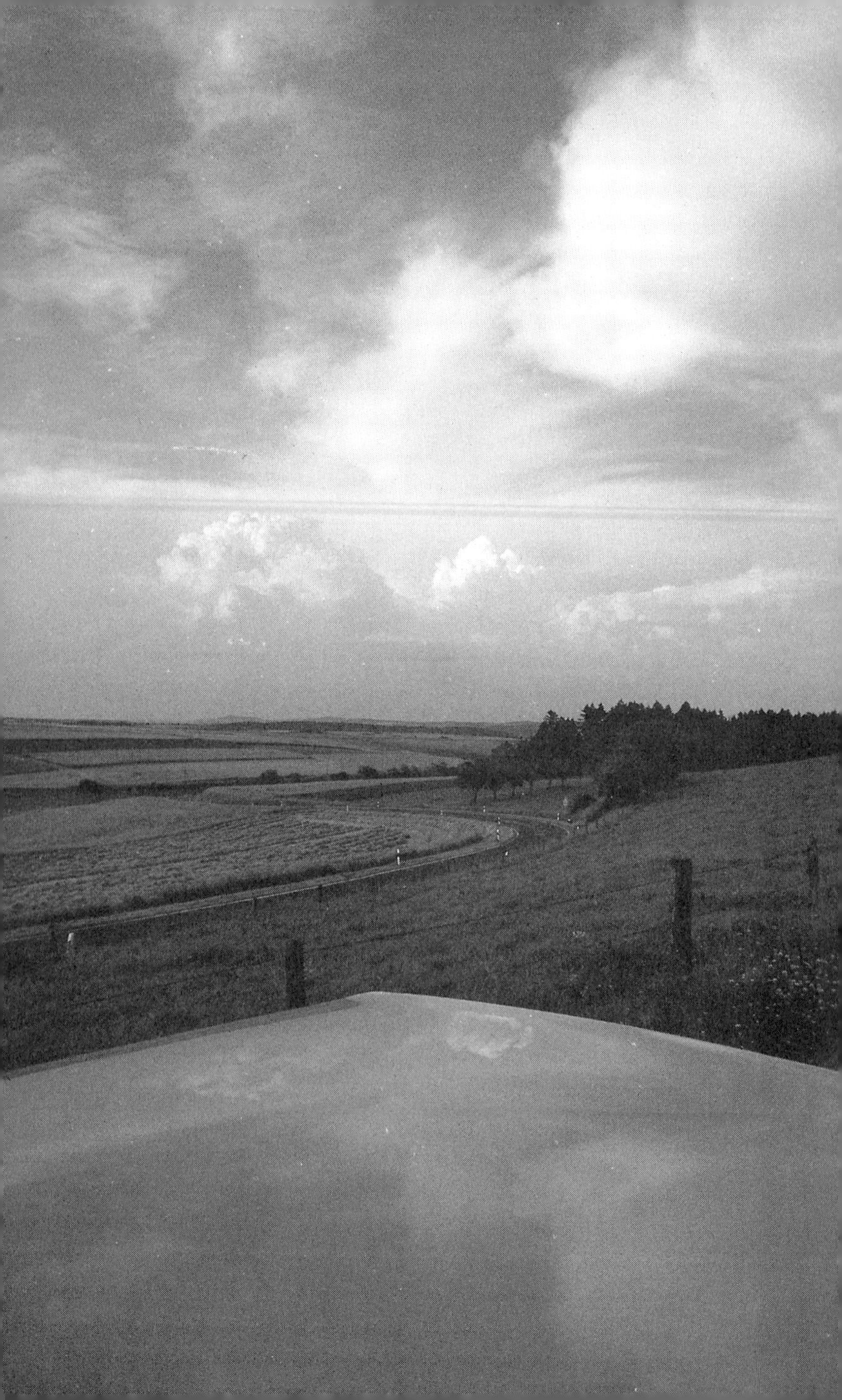

Pentax in the Forefront

"Asahiflex" was the name of the first Japanese 35mm SLR camera. It appeared in 1952 and 35 years on this new autofocus 35mm reflex camera, the Pentax SFX, comes from the same stable; the Asahi Optical Co. Ltd. of Tokyo. These two cameras encompass the entire range of technical achievement in camera construction by the Asahi team of development engineers. Many of their innovations have become standard features in 35mm SLR cameras. One notable example is the world's first instant-return mirror that was first introduced in 1954 in the Asahiflex II.

The Pentax Spotmatic was the first camera with through-the-lens metering. The abbreviation TTL is now a term which features in the specifications of most SLR cameras. The aperture-priority mode of exposure control, where the photographer preselects the aperture value, is now a standard feature in many SLR cameras. It was incorporated for the first time in the Pentax ES model of 1971. Five years later Asahi Optical further surprised the world by producing two of the smallest and lightest 35mm SLR cameras made up to that time – the Pentax ME and MX. The next achievement to add to this impressive record was the highly-professional Pentax LX with its unique combination of mechanical and electronic shutter control.

Then the Asahi team wrote the introductory chapter to today's saga of camera technology – autofocus – by introducing the ME-F. This camera, with its specially developed SMC 35-70mm, f/2.8 AF Zoom lens was the very first autofocus in SLR cameras. Because of the state of the art of electronics in cameras at the time, the circuits for metering control and focusing functions were in the camera. The

Landscape photography at dusk always involves some uncertainty. The foreground may appear too dark, but in this shot it is counterbalanced by the clouded sky.
Photo: Richard Hünecke

focusing motor, gearings and power supply had to be accommodated in a housing beneath the lens. This camera was clearly an intermediate step towards the present-day design of the Pentax SFX. Having the metering and control functions in the camera and the autofocus motor in the zoom lens, meant that electronic distance metering could be used with all other Pentax SMC lenses between 24mm and 300mm, with of course manual focusing. The K-bayonet too, introduced in 1975, proved to be a far-sighted decision and capable of further development. The five contacts connecting the autofocus motor in the lens with the electronic control in the Pentax ME-F body could be easily accommodated in its broad flange ring. Both of these features in a somewhat modified form are still present in the SFX. However, behind them lies completely new technology and new constructional features.

This short resumé of the technical innovations from Asahi Optical emphasises one basic principle. All the ideas were developed to facilitate the photographer's work and aspirations; to help him overcome difficulties and uncertainties, and to do this effectively. Against the background of this Pentax philosophy we will not be surprised to find that the introduction of the new autofocus camera has not suddenly made the previous systems obsolete and outmoded. On the contrary, the underlying design brief confirms that the introduction of new technology for its own sake, whether in electronics or lenses, is not the decisive factor in the company's forward-thinking, development-conscious policy. No, this aspect is determined at the interface between camera and system components, in the intricate connections present in the bayonet between lens and camera, in order to allow future developments within the system.

In retrospect I must say that the Asahi engineers must have been guided by a lucky star when they developed the K-bayonet in 1975. This was still totally suitable in 1983 to accommodate in its broad flange ring the six electrical contacts for the new system. Electronic transfer ensures fast and reliable communication of data between camera and lens, particularly for the multiple-program mode with its six exposure programs, better and faster than any type of mechanical transfer would ever be able to achieve.

K – KA – KAF – The Logical Progression

Electronic data transfer from the SMC-A lenses to the Pentax SFX body is the essential feature in the new autofocus system. The camera needs a considerable amount of lens information. Two seemingly minor additions, hiding a considerable technical effort, raised the KA bayonet to the autofocus KAF bayonet. A seventh contact is the key to the ROM data chip which stores data for Pentax AF-lenses, and the mechanical coupling that connects the autofocus motor in the SFX camera with the helical gear in the AF lens provides the drive. The incorporation of the KA information transfer paths between lens and camera into the autofocus design of the Pentax SFX enabled the life of the K/KA bayonet to be extended, although with the addition of the two extra features which distinguish the new Pentax SFX autofocus system. The "K" in the bayonet description assumes a new meaning for today's Pentax owner: it is the common element between the "old" – in the chronological, not the technological sense – and the "new" for the autofocus system.

All lenses with a bayonet bearing the letters "K" or "KA" will fit on the new Pentax SFX camera. Naturally, these lenses will not allow you to use the autofocus facility – at least not directly. Such lenses will be able to use the exposure programs available on the camera insofar as they possess the necessary contacts in the bayonet ring. I have devoted several chapters of the book to this theme and shall not discuss it further at this point. On the other hand, the new Pentax AF lenses will fit onto any LX, Super-A, or P30 Pentax camera, or even on one of the classic models such as the ME or K2, and they can be used with all the automatic functions for which those particular cameras are designed. The Pentax AF lenses have a ring for manual focusing and the familiar aperture ring with the A-position by the highest f/number on the ring. Therefore it is not necessary to take a re-training course to shoot alternately with Pentax A or AF lenses on the SFX, or when using another K-bayonet Pentax camera with one of the new AF lenses.

I consider this an excellent solution because the photographer who already possesses and likes one of the earlier Pentax cameras is able to extend his equipment with the new autofocus camera instead of discarding it. Because of the decision to retain the continuity of the Pentax system, which meant retaining the bayonet, the Asahi engineers decided against miniature drives in the lens and instead placed the autofocus motor within the camera body. This may become the standard in autofocus technology, but it is a topic that is still widely discussed amongst camera enthusiasts. A well-known competitor of Asahi introduced their AF system, more or less at the same time, which incorporates the motor and gearing in the lens. This needed a completely new bayonet construction, thereby creating an entirely new camera system.

There is another argument to be considered. Why introduce an expensive drive unit into each lens if it is just as easy to achieve the same result by installing a slightly larger, simpler, and maybe less delicate, drive unit in the camera? Whether one system, with comparable lenses, manages to obtain perfect focusing one tenth of a second faster than the other is more of an academic point then a practical one. After all, we are talking of times in the region of 0.4 to 0.8 seconds for the entire focusing range from infinity to close-up. As it is, the small clutch between the AF motor and the lens performs its duty perfectly and reliably, and that's what counts!

If you are worried that after years of use, wear in the mechanism might lead to less precision, then you can put your worries aside. After the motor has performed its focusing action the autofocus computer checks whether the part of the subject within the focusing area is properly focused. If not, it will quickly impart a correction to the AF motor. Because it does not base its conclusions on the revolutions of the motor, but on the image received at the AF sensor, it is not susceptible to errors occurring along the mechanical chain: AF motor – lens – helical gear. This takes us straight into the depths of autofocus technology.

If we consider the basic concept of the Pentax SFX system we recognize that it is not really a compromise in the true sense of the word. The conception of any autofocus SLR camera, and this includes the Pentax SFX, is always a decision arising from production constraints and a decision as to whether to go for the best possible level of technology at a given time or for continuity with earlier systems. Personally I would prefer the advantages and opportunities arising from continuity because as a user I am better served in utilising my resources and experience by a proven system.

An improved model of the SFX, called the SFX_N, has some additional valuable features. The most important is the automatic exposure bracketing system. Operation of the camera remains the same, although the layout of the displays in the CENTIC panel has been changed to accommodate the symbol for exposure bracketing. Other valuable features are a 1/4000 sec. top shutter speed, illumination for the LCD panel and a multi-frame mode for the self-timer. The Pentax SFX_N and where its operation differs from the SFX is described in the final chapter.

SFX – The SLR with the Bright Ideas

First acquaintance with the Pentax SFX confirms that it has a character exactly as its looks suggest. The photographer is informed clearly and concisely what it is capable of and what has to be entered and how it will react.

On further inspection, the right-hand side of the Pentax SFX warmly invites your grip. At first sight it may look somewhat heavy, but appearances are deceptive. The solid handgrip has a good confidence-inspiring feel. The handgrip, housing the power supply and film transport motor, is solid and affords a sturdy support. Beneath its smooth matt exterior, the camera body is made of die-cast aluminium and the front plate of die-cast zinc. Both are reinforced with bracing ribs and webs, and are very robust and stable. Even so, if you should use your SFX camera with the 3000g SMC Pentax-A 300mm f/2.8 ED/IF lens, don't carry the combination by the camera strap, but support it from the lens, because otherwise the weight will strain the bayonet. The same applies to the Pentax LX and the Super-A.

Without batteries the SFX body weighs 665g, a good weight to dampen slight camera shake at slower shutter speeds. It features two motors which do away with some internal mechanical couplings necessary in other forms of construction, making it 100g heavier than the slightly smaller Pentax LX which is renowned for its extreme robustness. However, you may be confident the SFX is also a most sturdy construction.

Should we regret the passing of classical camera design? The matt-silver chrome or black upper section and the leather-look cover? I am not sure. The oblique contours and softly rounded corners and edges of the SFX body could have equally well been fashioned in die-cast metal. But the self-supporting, rigid shaped sections that the SFX has on top of its die-cast shell have other points in their favour. If you carry your camera

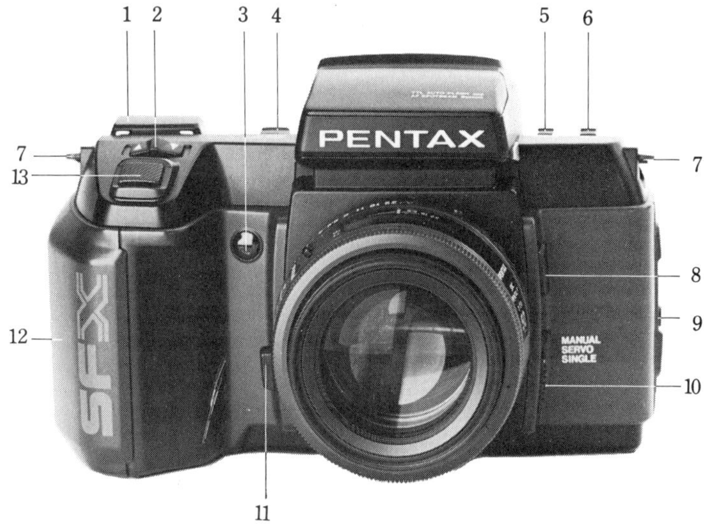

1 Hot shoe with cover
2 Selector switch for input of shutter speed, data, and program selection
3 LED display for self-timer
4 Main switch
5 Selector switch for exposure programs and shooting frequency
6 Selector switch for film speed and exposure compensation
7 Lug for carrying strap
8 Release socket
9 Back panel release
10 Autofocus selector switch
11 Lens release button
12 Compartment for lithium battery
13 Shutter release

into crowded places you will not be able to avoid the occasional knock which on a brass or die-cast zinc case could result in a more or less severe dent. A large dent could seriously interfere with the finely-tuned functioning of the mechanical or electronic interior. The outer plastic casing of the SFX cushions impact and furthermore will only show perhaps a small scratch on the exterior to remind you of the incident. Even so, be careful because a serious impact could cause damage to the functioning of the SFX.

Because of its distinctive shape and finish, the SFX sits pleasantly in your hand, never feeling slippery even in the most

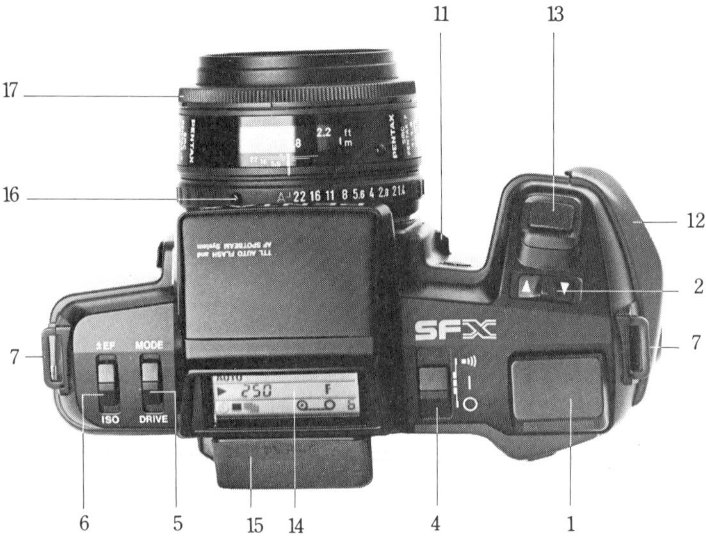

1 Hot shoe with cover
2 Selector switch for input of shutter speed, data and program selection
4 Main switch
5 Selector switch for exposure programs and shooting frequency
6 Selector switch for film speed and exposure compensation
7 Lug for carrying strap
11 Lens release button
12 Compartment for lithium battery
13 Shutter release
14 CENTIC information panel
15 Soft rubber eye cup
16 Locking button for A-position of aperture ring
17 Manual focusing ring

humid conditions. The ergonomic profile for palm and thumb ensure a safe grip with the right hand only, even if it is fitted with the 880g AF 300mm f/4.5 ED/IF lens.

Three Things to do to get You Started

First action: attach the lens to the camera. Align the red dot on the flange of the KAF lens bayonet with the one on the camera

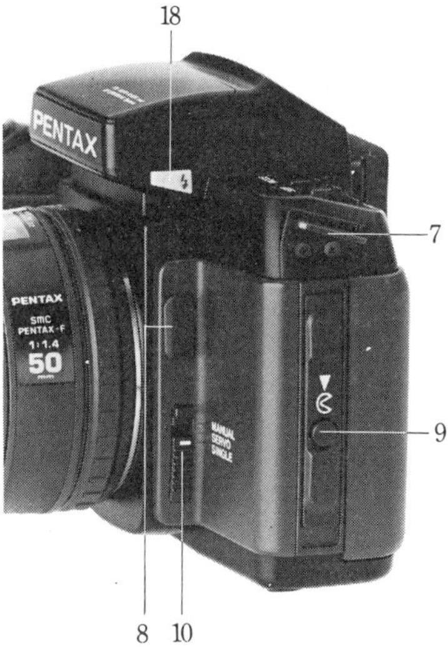

7 Lug for carrying strap
8 Release socket
9 Back panel release
10 Autofocus selector switch
18 Flash pop-up button

bayonet ring. Insert the lens into the camera's lens mount and turn it clockwise until it locks with a click. The lens can be turned in one direction only: when turning it you may feel a slight vibration in your fingertips. This is not a mechanical fault, but due to some ball bearings in the bayonet rings – a speciality of the KAF technology that we shall learn more about in the next chapters.

Second action: load the film, or more precisely, let the camera do it for you. To do this, open the back by sliding down the back cover release catch while simultaneously depressing the back cover lock button. Insert the film cassette, upper part first, into the film chamber with the DX-information pins, and pull the film leader across as far as the orange marker, making sure that the film is completely flat, and then close the back. If the main switch is set to position I, then the camera will wind the film to the first frame. If the main switch is set to "0" then it will wait until it is set to "I" to perform the film winding. Should you have pulled the film further than the orange marker,

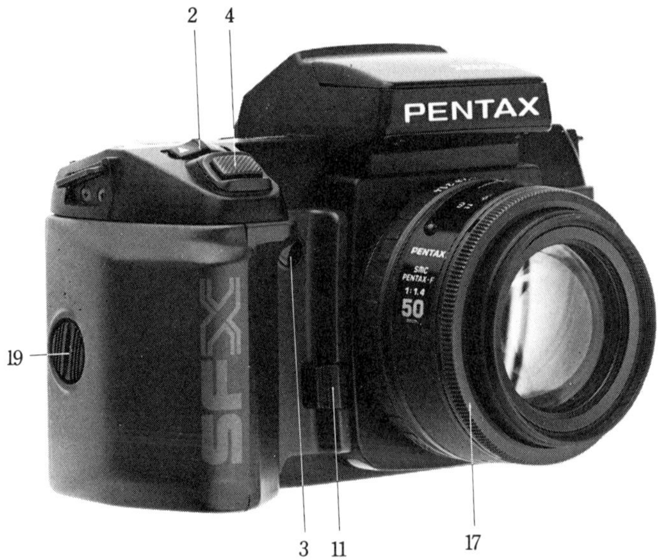

2 Selector switch for input of shutter speed, data and program
3 LED display for self-timer
4 Main switch
11 Lens release button
17 Ring for manual focusing
19 Battery compartment screw

then you can thread the excess one or two centimetres into the narrow slit between the take-up spool and the camera housing. If the end is longer than this, you should remove the cassette from the chamber, rewind the film back into the cassette a little and start again. More about DX-coding and what to do if your film is not DX coded is given in the section "Traffic Rules for the Four-in-Hand".

Third action: Program selection from the four basic program modes available on the SFX. Turn the aperture ring to "A", lightly press on button "C" next to the eyepiece, and close the autofocus selector switch at the bottom left of the lens mount to SINGLE: your SFX is now ready.

Even if the main switch is set at "0", the SFX will inform you

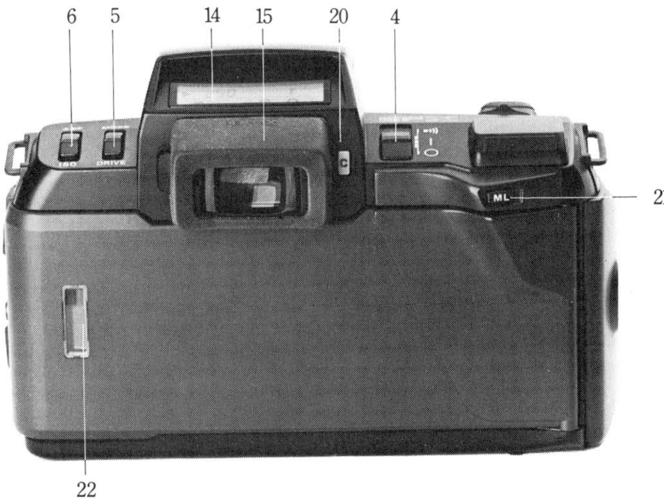

4 Main switch
5 Selector switch for exposure programs and shooting frequency
6 Selector switch for film speed and exposure compensation
14 CENTIC information panel
15 Soft rubber eye cup
20 C-button for fast change to program mode
21 Exposure mode button
22 Film cartridge window

in the large CENTIC display panel of what is being selected. PROGRAM will be displayed in the top line, to the right of that the variation of program mode suitable for the lens attached. The second line is reserved for exposure data and appears only after the main switch has been set to "I" and you have lightly pressed the release button to obtain a reading. Towards the left-hand corner of the lower line is a single square: this indicates single frame shooting and is always selected when button "C" next to the eyepiece is pressed. The DX code indicates that the camera has read the film speed into its memory from the code on the cassette. The film advance symbol to the right of the DX value indicates that a film is loaded. This can be checked by looking through the film information window at the back of the camera. The display in the right-hand corner of the lower line is the number of the next frame, so this will be number 1 for a freshly loaded film. The frame counter counts to 99.

Now that your SFX is fully programmed for your first set of pictures you can begin shooting with confidence, knowing that all your shots will be correctly exposed, provided they are not taken in unusual lighting conditions or the subjects have extreme contrast. Your pictures will also be correctly focused, again providing you have not chosen, for example, to take a speeding motorbike whizzing past you at close range. The sharpness and brilliance of your pictures will be excellent, provided the ambient lighting conditions and the speed of your film have allowed sufficient scope for the program mode to choose shake-free shutter speeds. Too many restrictions for such an expensive fully automatic camera, I hear you say? Don't be disappointed. The Pentax SFX will do everything you ask of it, provided the circumstances allow it full rein. But if you leave the important decisions and modes of functioning to a computer that is bound by pre-programmed parameters, then you will come across unexpected results from time to time. In order to help you cope with subjects that are not straightforward the Pentax SFX has three other exposure programs as well as a fully-manual mode that should be suitable for any conceivable situation.

Lithium Batteries and Other Alternatives

You need not worry about the power supply for your first twelve films. When you buy the camera it is supplied with a lithium battery Type BR-P 2 P-6 V, which is located in the hand grip. Its capacity should be sufficient for 37 films of 36-exposures, provided you do not use the built-in mini-flash. If you use the flash for about half of your exposures, then the battery should last for about 600 shots, or 16, 36-exposure films. These figures will only be achieved if the battery was in good condition when bought and you have not left it for a long time, but we can never be sure that a battery in a shop is fresh and it is advisable to think about the question of power supply after about 10 films. Lithium batteries have a high capacity, or yield, and they remain capable of delivering sufficient power even in low temperatures. They may also be stored for long periods, even if partially spent. However, this type is the most expensive energy source for your SFX and they are not

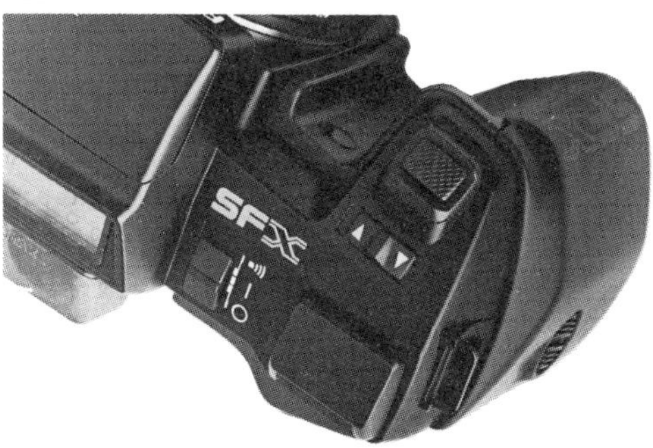

The flat battery compartment cover with 6V lithium battery is supplied with the camera

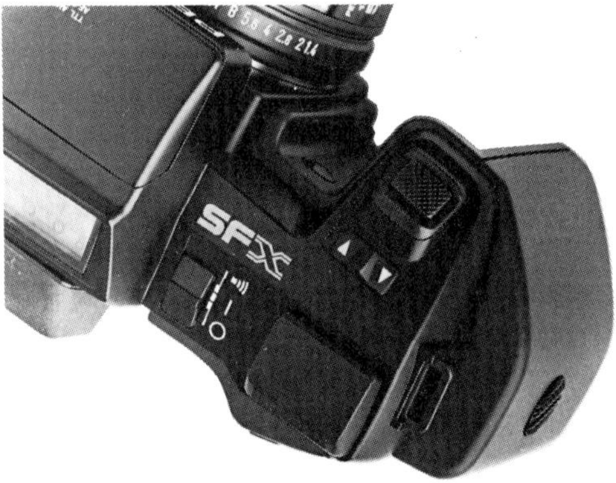

The battery compartment cover with four alkaline batteries makes the SFX longer by 0.5cm. These batteries are easier to find and are cheaper.

available everywhere. In rural areas and many holiday resorts the chances of obtaining lithium batteries are slim, so you should always carry a spare battery if your journey is likely to be longer than 10 films.

Alternatively you could order with your SFX the "AA" Battery Grip SFX. This holds four alkaline batteries AA size or LR6. This increases the length of the camera by half a centimetre, but you will be less restricted as far as batteries are concerned. Alkaline batteries of this type are available almost everywhere and, provided they are fresh, will also last for about 1300 exposures or 37, 36-exposure films (without flash). Using the flash for every other shot, the alkaline batteries will supply enough power for 650 shots or 18, 36-exposure films. Most supermarkets and petrol stations sell these batteries at very reasonable prices. Whatever you do, don't use rechargeable batteries in your Pentax SFX.

To conclude the topic of power supply. Polar explorers, Alpine climbers, winter sports enthusiasts and reporters working in the rarified cold air of the high Alps need the Remote Battery Pack F and the Terminal Grip F, connected via a 1m long cable, which is screwed to the camera in place of the standard grip. The battery pack holds four alkaline batteries, AA size/LR6, and is best kept under the parka and pullover in a warm pocket close to your body. Kept warm in this way, the batteries will supply the camera with sufficient power, even in the most severe winter conditions.

The Pentax SFX has no special button for checking the state of the battery. The electronic processor will check this every time the camera is switched on and every time the release is pressed. If the voltage drops below a certain level, then the battery symbol in the CENTIC display panel will blink. This means that you need to obtain a new set of batteries soon. Under most circumstances the batteries will be good for another one or two films.

The E2PROM memory chip in the processor of the Pentax SFX retains the data even when the batteries are being changed. The SFX therefore requires no separate back-up battery for storing this data.

One Ring and Two Dual-purpose Switches

The number of operating elements needed to control the seven types and variations of exposure modes on the SFX are surprisingly few. Altogether there are nine. One of these is the same aperture ring that is fitted to the A-lenses. Then there is a pair of dual-purpose switches, one on the battery compartment/handgrip, the other to the left of the CENTIC display panel. These two switch combinations are the main members of the input team. Compared with one or two other cameras of 1986 one thing is pleasantly surprising: the oft-criticized miniature buttons, requiring the fine touch of a brain surgeon, have been spared the Pentax SFX user. When the main switch is returned to "0" the camera is switched off but the display in the CENTIC panel remains visible, expect for the metered values.

The arrangement could not be more logical. The switch on the left provides the commands to the individual areas of the camera's computer. On the right, immediately behind the

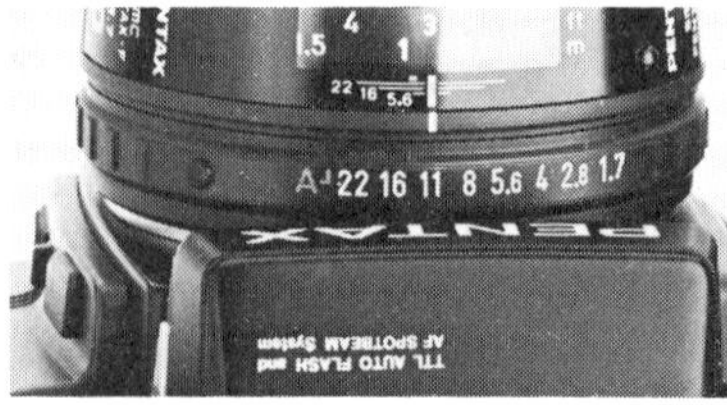

The aperture ring …

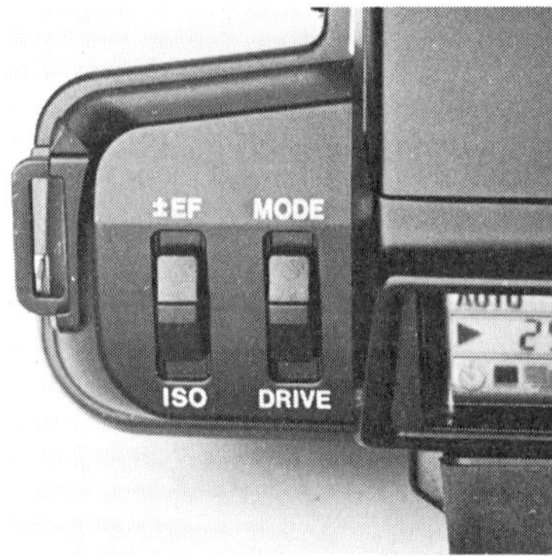

… two selector switches for shooting modes and film data …

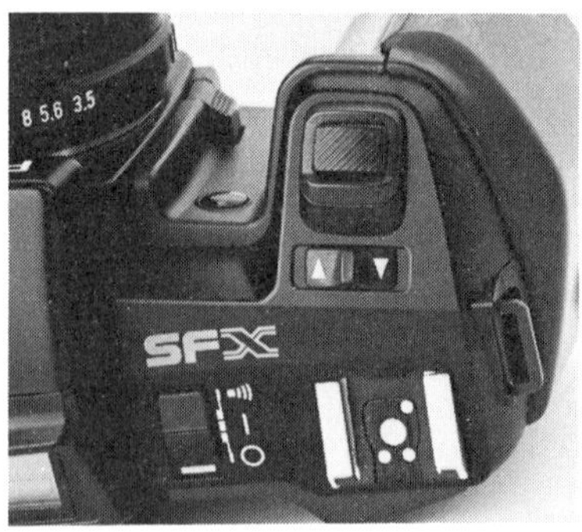

… and one selector switch between release button and main switch are sufficient to effect all functions to control your Pentax SFX.

release button, the select switch sets the exposure data. These two switches are sufficient for nearly all the commands that you may wish to enter. Between them, at the rear of the pentaprism and always in direct view of the photographer, is the CENTIC central information panel. The name is derived from CENTral Information Cluster and is a LCD panel arranged as three lines of data display.

The position MODE of the left-hand switch allows the selection of one of the individual variations in exposure control that are available through the select switch on the right. These are arranged in two logical groups. If the aperture ring of the AF lens is set to "A", you can select one of the three program modes or the shutter speed priority mode. It does not matter whether you push the select switch to the right or the left, the program cycle will run through the available modes either in the clockwise or anti-clockwise direction accordingly, displaying the selection in the CENTIC panel.

Stopping the cycle when AUTO is displayed in the upper line of the CENTIC panel on the left-hand side, allows selection of shutter speeds between $^1/_{2000}$ and 1 second if shutter speed priority mode is also displayed in the LCD panel. The select switch has no effect for all other positions in this cycle.

If the aperture ring is turned from the "A" position to an aperture value (f/number) then the aperture priority mode or the manual setting of shutter speeds may be selected via the MODE and select switches. In the AUTO position of this cycle the select switch remains without effect – provided the MODE switch has been returned to its centre position – because the aperture value is the only parameter that is manually selectable in this shooting mode, and this is done by turning the aperture ring on the AF-lens.

If you selected MAN to be displayed in the top line of the CENTIC panel, then two black arrows in the centre line will remind you that you have to select both the aperture value and the shutter speed. The shutter speed is always the value on the left in the centre line. Shutter speeds between $^1/_{2000}$ and 1 second may be selected. To select "100" when using an independent flashgun requiring a fixed shutter speed of $^1/_{100}$ second, or "bulb" for long exposures, operate the select switch while keeping the MODE switch pressed.

The DRIVE position of the left-hand switch is responsible for the self-timer and the two film transport speeds. Symbols

Ten contact pins at the bottom of the film cartridge chamber transfer the DX code on the film cartridge to the exposure control in the camera. The five contacts beneath the film guide provide electrical connection between the SFX and the Data Back.

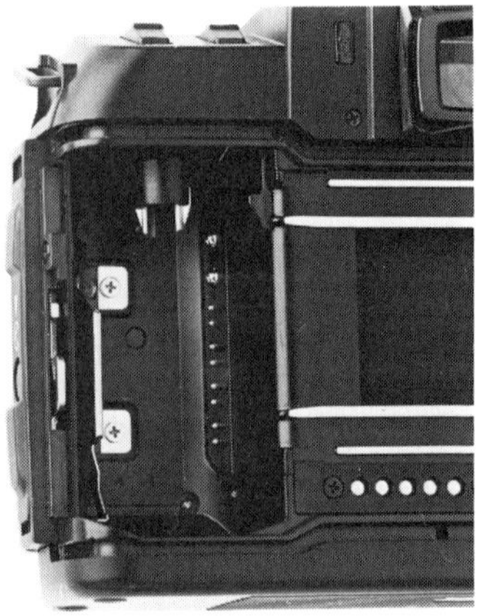

for these three options appear in turn on the LCD panel, as the select switch is pushed repeatedly to the right or left whilst the other switch is held at DRIVE. The cycle stops at the required option as soon as the select switch is released.

Only one switch for the film.

The other switch, further to the left, is the ISO/exposure-compensation switch which is responsible for film speed functions. Sliding this switch to the ISO position will bring the film speed display into the LCD panel. The speed is displayed in the centre line and will be either the automatically read-in value from the DX-coded film cassette or a manually-entered value. When the value is displayed you can change it by the select switch to a value between 6 and 6400 ISO. This allows manual input of film speed or the overriding of a pre-programmed value; in the latter case the "DX" in the bottom line will blink. The display returns to the exposure values as soon as the ISO switch is released.

When this switch is pushed to "+/- EF", this symbol followed by "+/-0.0", will normally appear in the centre line of the CENTIC panel. This indicates that the shutter speed/aperture combinations are the metered values and no

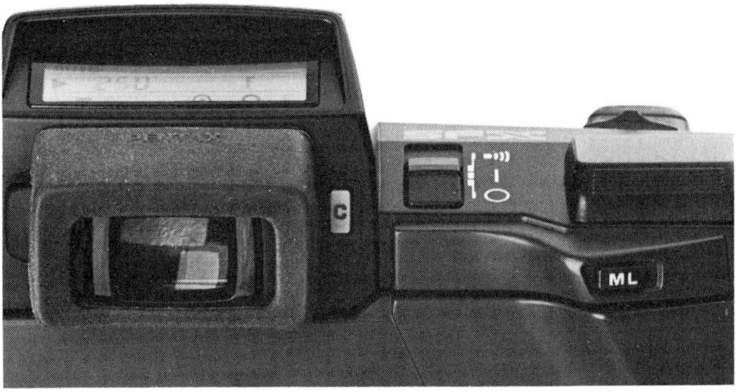

The C-button next to the eyepiece resets the SFX from any exposure and shooting mode to standard program mode and single frame frequency. The small but easily accessible ML button is to lock the metered exposure data.

compensation has been entered. When, why and by how much you should compensate the metered values is a very important topic concerning the combination of light, film, shutter speed and aperture and I will deal with it later on. By keeping this switch activated and simultaneously sliding the select switch to the left or the right, you are able to select compensation factors from +4 to -4 aperture stops in half-stop steps. The constantly blinking "+/- EF" symbol between the exposure values displayed in the CENTIC panel and in the viewfinder serves to remind you that you have selected a compensation factor.

Four Buttons for Special Functions

Four more buttons function independently of the select switch and activate less frequently required, but still very important, camera functions. A small, hardly noticeable button marked with a "C" in a grey panel is the exposure-mode clear button. It is situated to the right of the eyepiece where it can be reached easily with the right thumb. Press it lightly to:

○ Clear any previously-programmed shooting modes. The Pentax SFX then returns to normal program mode.

- ○ Return to aperture priority mode if an aperture value has been selected on the AF-lens;
- ○ Cancel any programmed exposure compensation factor;
- ○ Return film transport mode from continuous to single frame shooting;
- ○ Cancel the self-timer function if it has been selected, or stop it once the count-down has started.

The button marked "ML" is also within reach of the right thumb. This is the exposure memory lock button and pressing it will retain the currently metered exposure data, for a number of shots if desired. This can be useful if you want to use an exposure value obtained for a particular frame, let's say looking obliquely downwards at a scene, for another shot looking obliquely upwards, or if you wish to retain the same exposure value for a series of shots. The "ML" button may also be used if you want to use the Pentax SFX as an exposure meter. You point it at the subject without looking through the viewfinder and check the exposure data in the CENTIC panel whilst pressing the "ML" button. If the aperture ring is not set to the "A" position, then the aperture value will not be displayed in the CENTIC panel. Should the aperture value blink in the panel, then this means that the required value cannot be selected as it is not available on the lens.

The third function may be found at the base of the SFX. A slide switch, locked by a safety button, activates motor and gearing for rewinding the film. Action will not occur if the main switch is set to "0" but as soon as the main switch is returned to "I" the rewinding process will spring into action and cannot then be stopped, not even by the main switch. The motor returns the film completely into the cassette. The processing labs don't need the film leader, but if you want to process your own films you will need it to thread the film into the developing tank. The film leader is also useful if you wish to exchange a partially-exposed film for another, also partially-exposed film. In this case you will have to obtain a film leader retriever. I have one made by Hama and it has always performed the job for me. Ilford also supply one.

The fourth member of the quartet is the SINGLE/SERVO/MANUAL selector switch at the front left of the lens mount which controls the individual modes of electronically selected focusing. What happens there is the fascinating topic of the chapter "SAFOX Takes Care of Focusing".

CENTIC and the Select Switch

The select switch follows a very clear logic in all the various functions connected to the central computer of the Pentax SFX. Sliding it to the left, i.e. towards CENTIC panel, decreases shutter speeds, increases ISO values or exposure compensation factors. On sliding the switch to the right the appropriate values are changed in the opposite direction. Keeping the switch depressed at the limit stop causes the values or symbols to run through the display at a rate of one every half second. In the program mode selection cycle the choice of modes is displayed in a correspondingly endless cycle in the upper line of the display. Sliding the select switch to the left the cycle will be displayed running to the left, sliding it to the right will cause it to change to the opposite direction. The same applies to the symbols of the three DRIVE functions which are displayed in the bottom line of the CENTIC panel.

The layout and design of the switches is clear and logical. However, they are not very easy to use if you are wearing thick gloves. An old and well-tried trick, used by hardened explorers of cold regions, is to wear a pair of thin cotton gloves inside the warm mittens. When you need to use the camera, simply remove the mittens. The thin gloves will be no hindrance to using the controls on the camera but they will afford some protection against the cold for the short time your hands are exposed.

Unlike other cameras, the information in the CENTIC display panel remains visible, even if the main switch is set to "0". Only the exposure data metered by the camera and displayed in the centre line will be extinguished. These reappear when the release is lightly pressed, provided the main switch has been set to "I", and they remain visible for about 12 seconds. The information displayed in the CENTIC panel is arranged in three lines. In the top line are the symbols and descriptions of the exposure programs. The second line shows the exposure data, an indication of whether an exposure compensation has been selected and, if appropriate, the programmed film speed. The third line keeps you informed of the type of film transport, self-timer functions and count-down times, the frame number, and, if the "DX" blinks, an indication that the automatically read-in film speed had been manually changed.

However, the CENTIC panel does not inform you of the selected autofocus functions, or about the built-in flashgun, or about the TTL control for the flash. This information may be found beneath or alongside the viewfinder image. From the wealth of information displayed in the CENTIC panel, only the symbol for the selected shooting mode, the shutter speed, and the "+/- EF" symbol (to remind you of any set exposure compensation) is shown in the viewfinder. This subdivision of information is logical and in keeping with practical applications. What is needed in the viewfinder before releasing the shutter is the shutter speed, to check whether it is adequate for shots free from camera shake for the particular subject, and the confirmation that the subject is properly focused.

Motive Power and Ways of Starting

The astonishing miniaturization that is now possible with motors and other components enables motorized film transport to be incorporated within the camera. The Pentax SFX, with its two motors is smaller, lighter and handier than any other Pentax camera with attached winder or motordrive.

The film transport motor may be set to one of two operating modes by the DRIVE switch and the select switch. In the

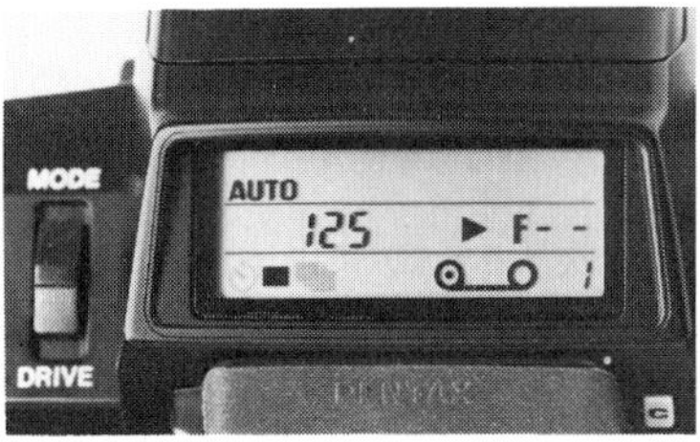

The little square in the lower line of the CENTIC panel indicates single frame shooting

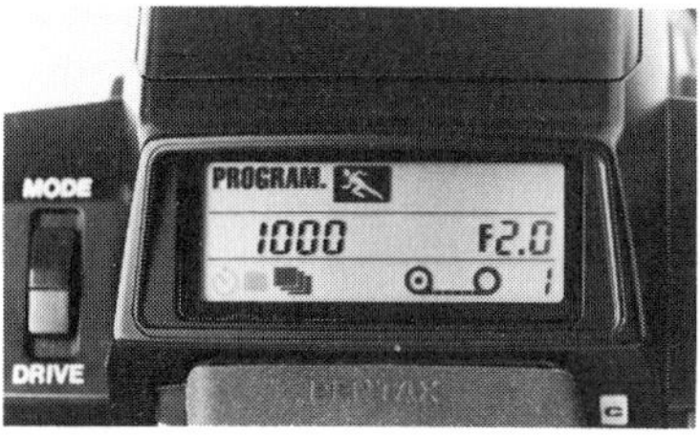

The fan symbol indicates continuous shooting at a rate of approximately 2 frames per second.

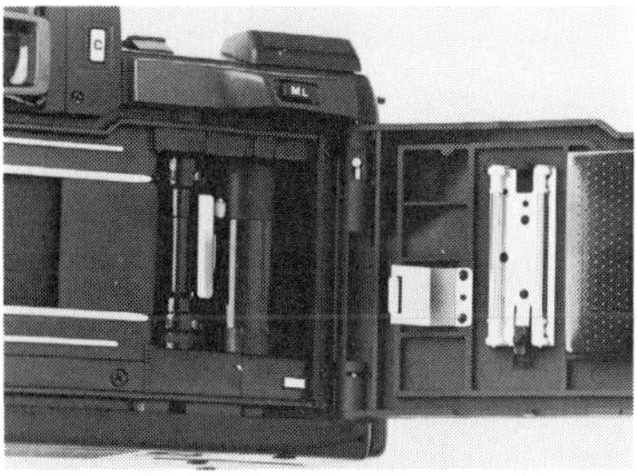

Little hooks and pads on the take-up spool and a system of pressure plates and guide rollers ensure automatic loading and precise film transport from one frame to the next.

single-frame shooting mode – a black square in the bottom CENTIC line – the SFX will make one exposure every time the shutter release is pressed. To take the next shot you have to let go the release button and press it again. If the processor has to make none, or only slight changes from the previous shot, then it is possible to shoot at a rate of 1 frame per second. This means you are fast enough for the majority of subjects and situations, but not for all.

When the symbol for continuous shooting – a "fan" of squares – is displayed in the bottom line of the CENTIC panel then the motor transport is switched to continuous, allowing series shots of 2 frames per second for as long as the shutter release is kept pressed. If you get carried away with the action unrolling in front of your SFX you will use up the entire film after 20 seconds. Whether you would be successful with a barrage of shots in say catching a diver at exactly the moment her fingertips break the surface of the water, remains doubtful. Your chances are 50:50. Either you catch that dream shot, or not. The success rate is determined by whether the half-second "long" interval between shots covered the critical moment or not. A lot can happen in half a second.

For example, go out and take some photographs on a late afternoon when the light is fading and the headlights of cars and buses are on. Put your SFX on a tripod, program it to shutter speed priority and select a shutter speed of $^1/_2$ sec. Now take a shot of a bus at the stop. The next shot exactly at the moment when it starts off. A third shot of the back of the bus moving away. The speed-blurred contours of these shots will demonstrate very clearly how difficult it is to catch a fast movement at exactly the right moment. The experienced professional photographer will use his camera in continuous shooting mode. However, he will have developed a feeling for when to depress the shutter to anticipate the right moment. Even with the fastest drive, the intermediate dark phase could be too long and the diver will have disappeared in a great splash. To master such situations you need a light and delicate finger on the trigger, a cool head and quick reactions. The response time of the SFX can be shortened by pre-focusing on a subject at more or less the correct distance, this will save the processor having to make large adjustments and the release command will be issued almost immediately.

An inexhaustible subject: man at work. The speed of the movements will determine whether you will set the SFX to AF-SINGLE, or AF-SERVO to save the trouble of constantly having to check correct focus and to be able to fully concentrate on picture composition. Taken with the AF 70-210mm Zoom.
Photo: Richard Hünecke

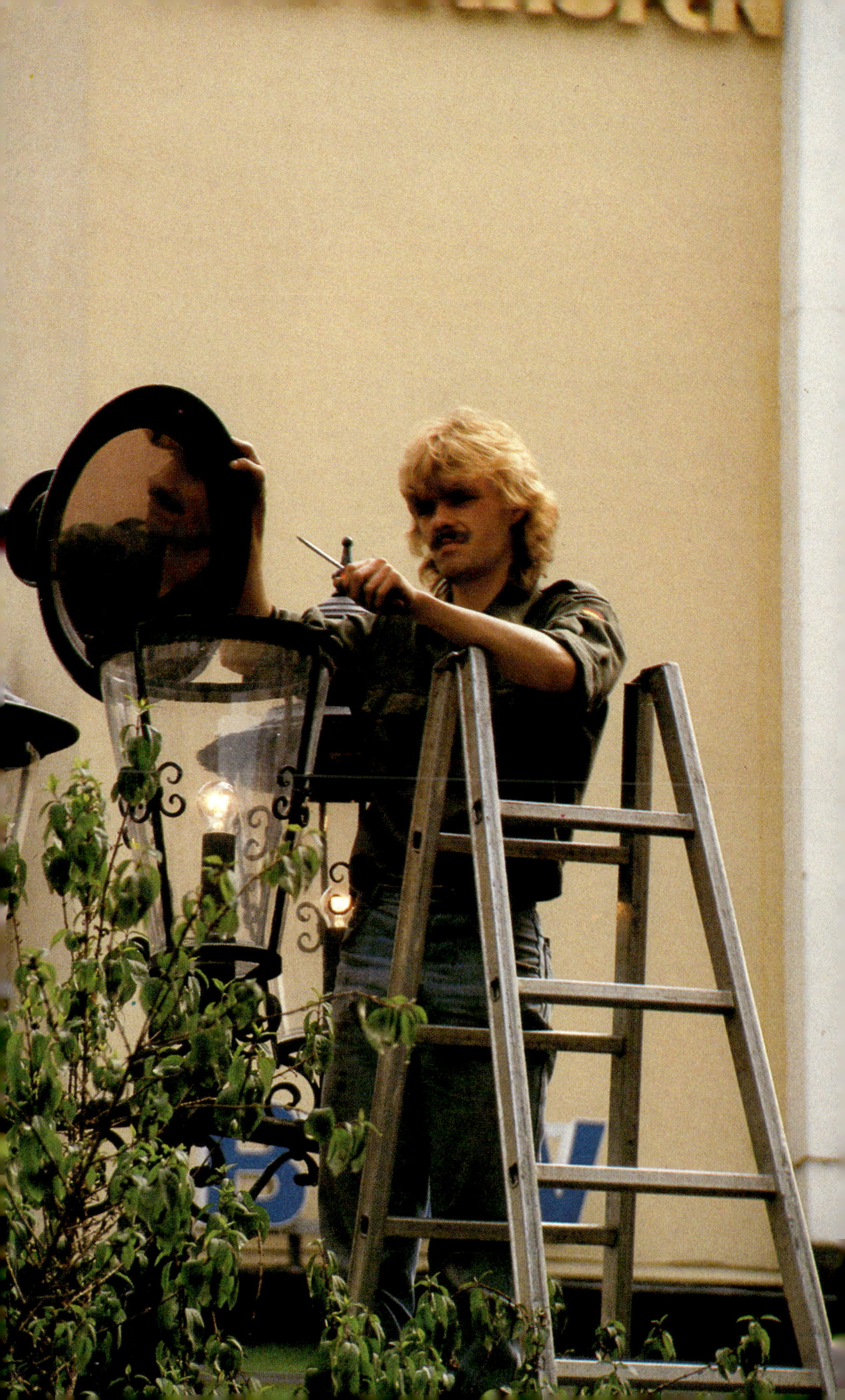

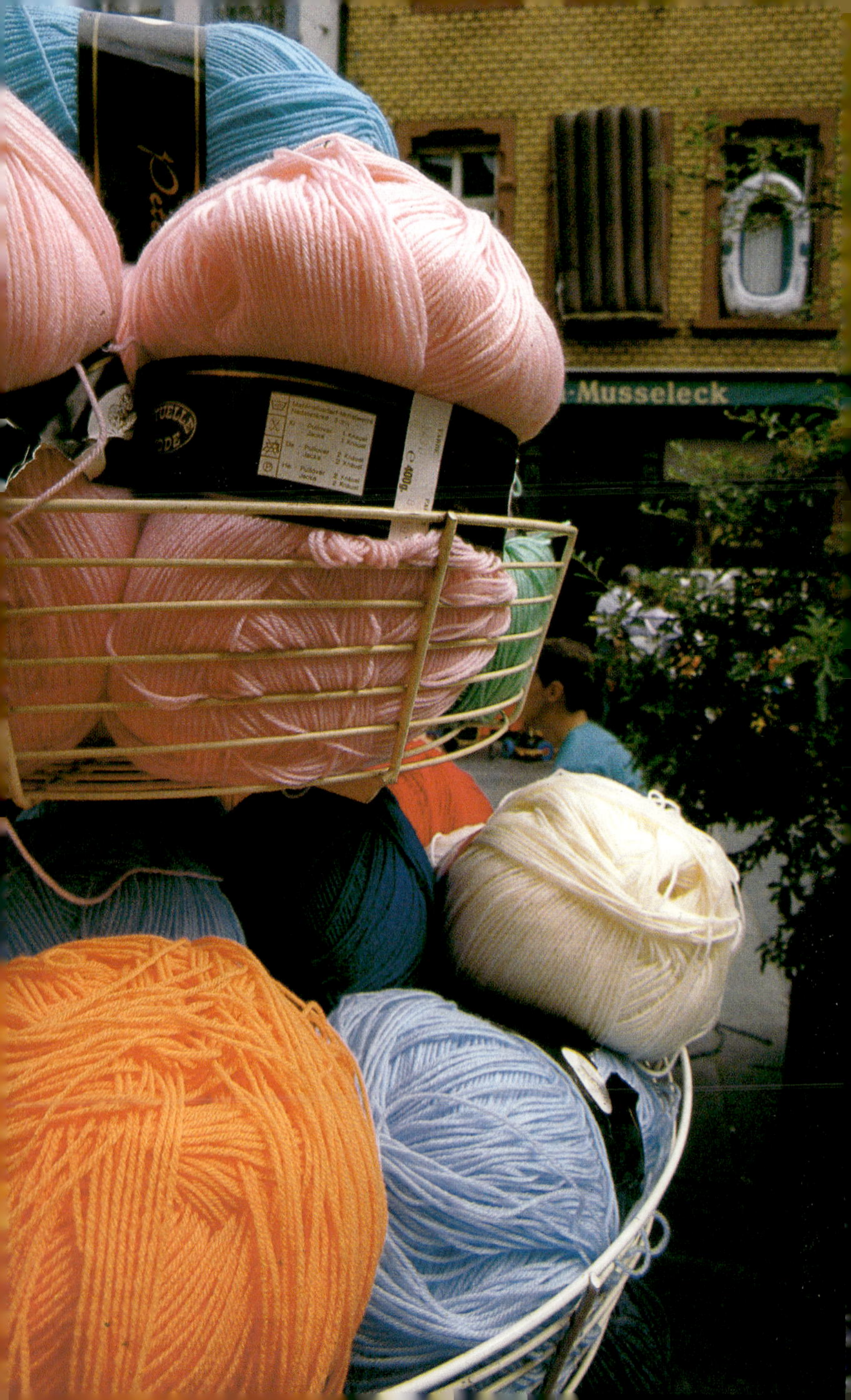
Musseleck

Starting: direct or indirect

The start command can be given in one of three ways. The shallow-grooved, non-slip release button starts the exposure metering and autofocus functions after it is pressed about half-way down, the shutter release is triggered at the very end of its travel. About a millimetre before its end stop is a pressure point which can be overcome easily by the finger without jarring the camera.

The second way of starting the shutter release process is by the self-timer. Its action is activated by simultaneously sliding the DRIVE switch and the select switch. The 12 seconds count-down period is started by pressing the shutter release. The self-timer function remains selected until it is cancelled by the selection of one of the two film transport modes via the DRIVE and Select buttons. The combination of self-timer and continuous shooting is impossible. It is illogical anyway. You can stop a count-down already underway by pushing the main switch from "I" to "0" (self-timer function remains selected), or by using the "C" button next to the eyepiece, or, of course, by the combination of DRIVE and Select switches. The last two possibilities cancel the self-timer function.

The self-timer is not just a little gadget to enable you to include yourself in the occasional group photograph. It can be more important as a release mechanism in cases where the SFX has calculated rather slow shutter speeds because of the lighting conditions and there would be a danger of camera shake if it was hand-held. If you are without a cable release, or you have left it at home, then with the camera on a tripod or some other firm support, release the shutter by the self-timer. A sometimes impossible condition is that your subject does not shift its position during the 12 seconds of count-down.

The camera has no remote release contact and you will look

To accommodate as much of a subject as possible in the frame is one reason for using short focal length lenses close to a subject. The other is to show the foreground greatly exaggerated in size against an insignificantly small background. *Photo: Richard Hünecke*

in vain for a conventional cable release socket. To trigger the shutter by flexible release you need the 1m long Cable Switch F. For connecting this to the camera the SFX has a three-pole socket – but there is nowhere to store the little cover when it is removed. Take good care and remember where you put it. These contacts should never be left exposed and you need to replace the cover immediately after use. The button on the Cable Switch F activates the metering and control functions of the SFX and starts the shutter in exactly the same way as the shutter release button, and it can be locked for long exposures.

Elegant technology exacts a price at times: double and multiple exposures are not included in the technical facilities of the SFX.

Traffic Rules for the Four-in-Hand

The four partners which, combined in the right way, will produce what we desire are the available light, the film speed, the setting of the shutter of the camera and the aperture of the AF lens. We want a correctly-exposed and sharp black-and-white or colour negative that will be perfect for enlarging, or colour slides suitable for projection. We want good colour saturation and contrast, but we may also want to convey a mood, put our own interpretation on the scene, or exaggerate some aspect. Insofar as all this can be controlled by the amount of light falling on the film in a certain time, the four partners are all we have to work with.

The first two embody the conditions presented to the camera, which cannot be influenced simply by pressing some button. We are left with the other two, with their interlocked effects, which are variable from shot to shot. In order that the shutter speed/aperture combination responds correctly, and according to the photographer's intent, to the prevailing conditions of light, film speed and subject, the "brain" controlling this foursome, be it the photographer himself or the exposure program, has to be aware in the first place of the effects and possibilities of the components determining these conditions.

The information concerning film speed is automatically logged in the camera's memory by the two single and four double contacts in the cassette chamber that read the ISO code from the black-silver patterns on the film cassette and pass it on to the microprocessor in the camera. Today there are only a few films on the market without DX coding – these are some special films and film that the photographer cuts himself from a large roll. If there is no DX coding, the ISO value must be entered manually by sliding the ISO switch and entering the value, via the select switch, which is then displayed in the centre line of the CENTIC panel. The SFX is programmed for

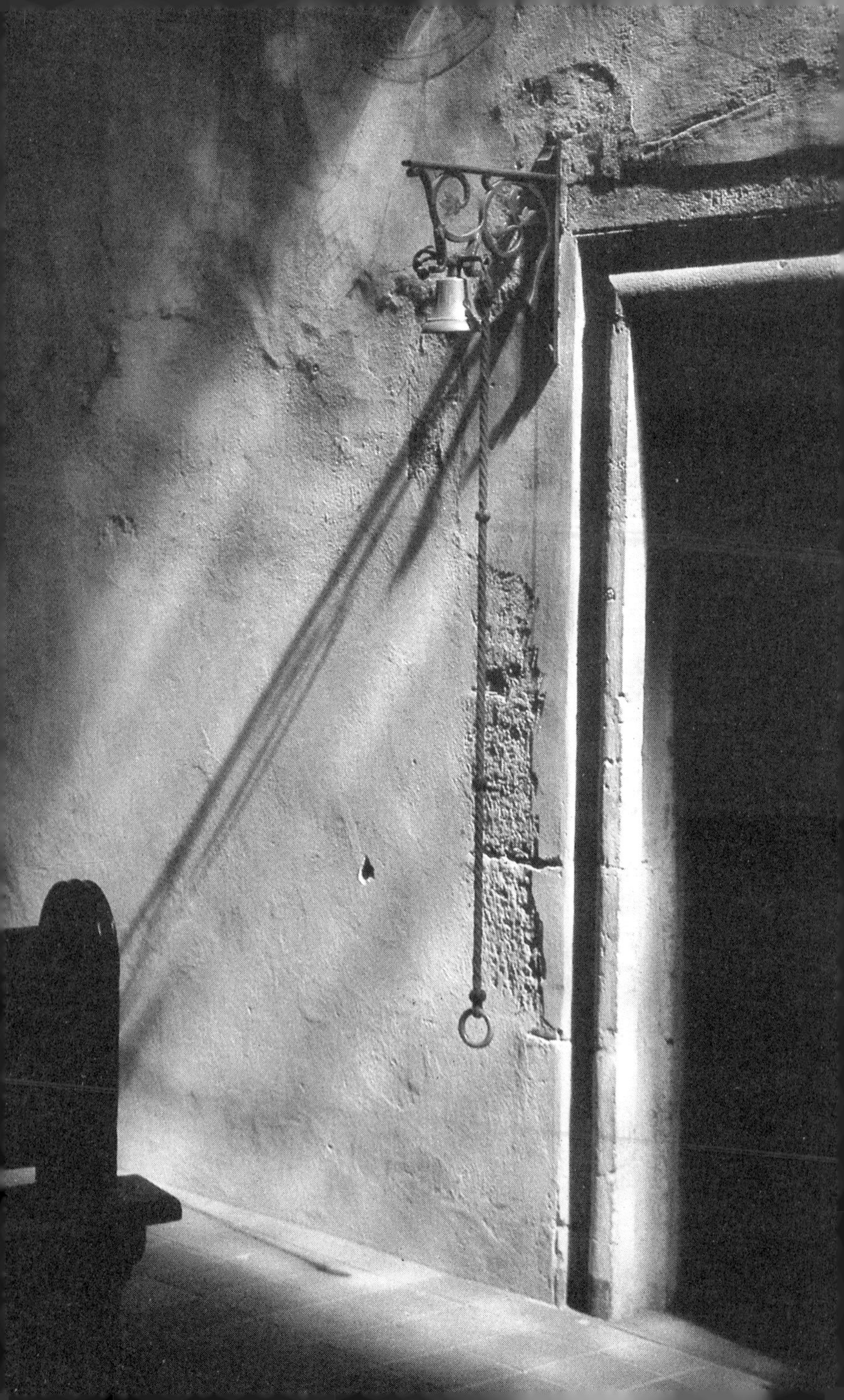

film speeds from ISO 25/15° to ISO 5000/38° for DX-coded films, and from ISO 6/9° to ISO 6400/39° for manual setting. Every time the ISO number is doubled or halved the film speed is twice or half that of the previous value. It is possible to override the automatically-programmed film speed by entering the required value manually. This has the effect of intentionally over- or underexposing that particular film. For example, it would be possible to overexpose young green foliage in spring to make it appear more delicate in the picture. Underexposure could be used to enhance an evening mood, or, for example, to lend a hint of drama to aircraft parked in the dusk.

Towards a Metered Value for Light

The light from the sun that falls onto our subject is reflected from the surfaces, structures and colours in very different ways. Photographically that is as far as the exposure of the picture is concerned, we need only consider the effect within the angle of view of the lens, i.e. the image projected onto the focusing screen of the Pentax SFX. Two GaAsP photo diodes "see" the brightness of the viewfinder image and transmit this as an electronic signal to the exposure processor. In order to fulfil its duty as the agent between the exterior conditions – amount of light from the subject – and the interior conditions – film speed – the processor will need a basis for comparison to evaluate this reading. Only then can it properly control the functions of shutter speed and aperture.

From the reactions of film emulsions to light and colours from the widest range of subjects a definition has been derived for an average or standard subject. What you should imagine under this term is difficult to define, but the essential point is that the standard subject is taken to reflect 18% of the incident light back in the direction of the camera. This value – known

Oblique lighting on old masonry is always effective. In this case I have not made any exposure compensation as I wanted to retain the strong contrast. AF 35-135mm Zoom.
Photo: Richard Hünecke

as average grey – has been taken as the universal standard for calibrating light-metering systems in photography. It always represents the average from all brightness variations within the subject. What such an average grey looks like can be seen on the very useful and much to be recommended Kodak Grey Card.

Luckily, film materials and the associated processing chemistry are quite tolerant. Two or three percentage points in the plus or minus direction can be easily accommodated. Subjects close to the 18% reflectivity standard are sun-tanned skin, wet sand, deep blue sky, red brick, spring-green foliage, and oranges. If the GaAsP colour diodes in the SFX metering system, or the cell in a hand-held exposure meter, "see" a subject that is composed mainly of these colours and reflectivity values, then the electronic metering system will calculate an exposure value that will produce the correct result as far as the reproduction of brightness and colours is concerned. The correct balance between shutter speed and aperture for this exposure value depends on the overriding decision of the photographer; the amount of light required for correct exposure is already calculated.

Our surroundings, and hence our photographic subjects, would be very monotonous were they all to consist of 18% average grey tones. Happily they are not and we have to deal with everything from brilliant white, reflectivity between 92-98%, and deepest black, reflectivity about 0.5%. These are the limit values for our range of photographic subjects. Dark, freshly-dug garden earth (*c*.5%); bright blue spring sky above (*c*.60%); dark bark of trees (*c*.10%); white, loose sand on the river bank behind the trees (*c*.50%); and a plank of freshly-sawn timber (*c*.35%) – these are examples of just some values to illustrate the variety of subjects we might encounter.

Black should stay black and white white

The variety of subjects is only the start of our problems with correct exposure, even for the very capable metering system

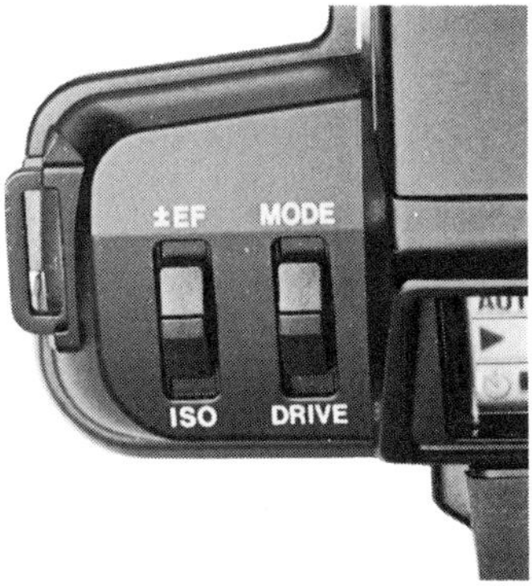

Exposure compensation is effected by the +/- button and the selector switch.

of the Pentax SFX. Despite their carefully selected colour sensitivity, and correction filters, the diodes "see" the most colourful subject only in terms of the grey scale, ranging from the very light to the darkest shades. They are incapable of analysing the subject details within their metering angle, but combine them to an average value which is then compared with the 18% average grey value. This is the basis to which everything is "reduced". This is what they are capable of, and nothing else. If the metering system perceives the brightness as too great, brighter than average grey, then it will indicate exposure values to suit. These will result in the white washed cottages in the bright Greek sunshine, or the brilliant white snow in the winter sun looking a muddygrey.

The electronic metering does not react any differently at the other end of the scale, only in the opposite direction. The metering processor will prescribe an extra long exposure time, with a large aperture, for a dark, polished wooden statue and produce a flat grey-toned statue instead of the rich dark-brown grain of the wood you wanted to record.

For both of these subjects the SFX has a solution, but it is the photographer who has to take the decision. Slide the switch marked "+/- EF" forward and operate the select switch until the CENTIC display shows a compensation value of between +1.0 to +1.5 for the white-on-white subject. This will result in an over-exposure of 1 or 1.5 f/stops and the white of the fishermen's cottages will remain white on the print or colour slide. The dark wooden statue, on the other hand, requires an exposure compensation of -1 to -1.5 to represent its deep colouring properly.

In both of these situations where lighting and subject deviate from the average, which are not as rare as you may think, you should do what most professional photographers would do. Take a sequence of shots, starting with a compensated shutter speed/aperture combination that corresponds to your experience, followed by two or three shots, each with a compensation factor of half-a-stop in the plus direction for the white-on-white situation. For the dark subject you program the exposure compensation in half stops in the minus direction. When the processed slides are returned you can select that which corresponds most closely to the result you had in mind when confronted with the subject. With colour prints on the other hand, if you send your films to one of the large processing labs, you may be disappointed to find that there is very little difference between the various exposures. The automatic printers used in the processing labs iron out such little differences to an average "good" print.

Touch-down on the contrast scale

This requires clear decisions by the photographer. Take a beach scene with colourful deck-chairs, cafe tables and umbrellas, white sails and hulls of boats, dark wooden gang-plank, with even darker structures underneath, all under a brilliant blue sky – the details seem simple, but what a trap for the unsuspecting photographer! The contrast from dark brown to brilliant white corresponds to a range of about 1:350. This is presented to the film which is expected to reproduce it all in fullest detail. In reality, to ensure that there is at least some detail in the darkest and in the lightest subject areas, we should not have a a contrast range of more than 1:32 for colour slide film.

If by chance you move the camera slightly to a different

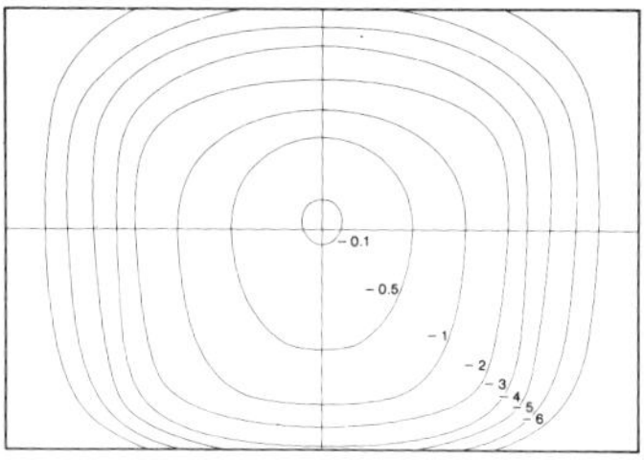

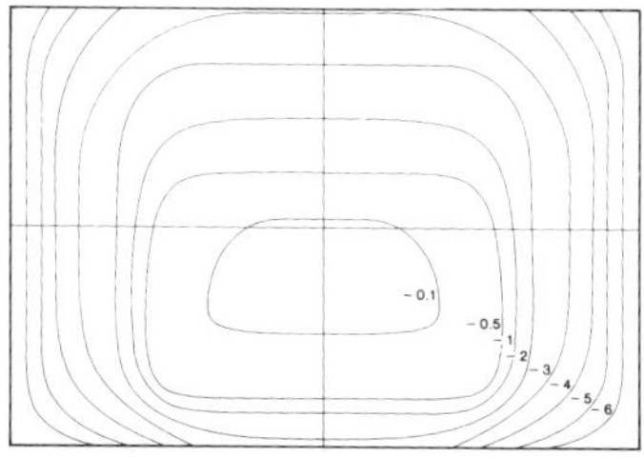

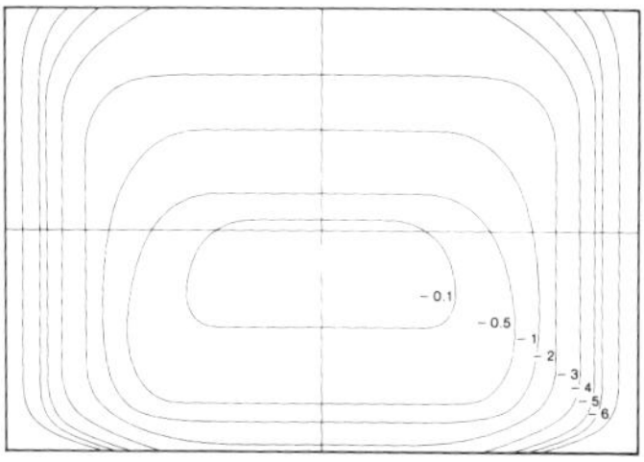

The metering system in the SFX is centre-weighted. The lines indicate how the contribution to the overall measurement decreases towards the edge of the frame.
Top left: SMC AF 50mm,f/1.4.
Top right: AF 35-70mm Zoom at 35mm setting
Bottom: AF 35-70mm Zoom at 70mm setting

section of the subject and the exposure meter system regards the average reflectivity now as 18%, then the painted tables, the green plants in the street cafe, and the path leading down to the beach, will be correctly reproduced because these are now at the centre of the contrast scale. The white sails, however, will be shown as blank white spaces without any detail, and the dark weathered wood will be just a black silhouette, perhaps with a few specks of light that reflection from the water has projected onto its surface. If the very dark and very light subject areas cover a small part of the frame and are placed more towards the edge of the picture, then their partially incorrect exposure would not be regarded as too detrimental.

If the exposure processor assesses the average luminance of a subject as clearly above the 18% calibration base, because the white sail covers a considerable part of the metering angle of the GaAsP photo diodes, then it will calculate much too high an exposure value. Then the white sail will be reproduced as dirty grey and the rest of the scene will be rather dull. If the dark wood covers a large section of the metering angle, because you chose a low shooting position to contrast the dark structure against the white sails in the background, then the resulting exposure value will be calculated as low. This is quite "normal" but does not represent reality, because the white sails will now be featureless white areas.

The same subject, the same light, but three different pictures. This exemplifies the essential question for the photographer – how do I measure what? The film's ability to accommodate contrasts dictates the answer. It will be necessary to decide on a suitable compromise. If the dramatic composition of the high triangular sails blowing in the wind against the static horizontal line of the beach are the intended expression of the picture, then the sails should cover a third, or at the most, just under half of the frame to obtain the correct exposure value. Metering the scene in this way you store the exposure value by pressing the "ML" button, re-align the frame to the desired section of subject and then, with the release still pressed half-way, allow the autofocus to complete its function, and then press fully down to take the shot. Following these steps, the background will be a little darker than it should be, but the sails will be shown in their full-blown whiteness, together with all their seams and details, outlined against a deep-blue sky that will lend your picture the special note that distinguishes it from the average snapshot.

Now let's turn our attention to the substructure of the gang-plank, crumbling and dark from constant beating of the waves, with a pattern of light moving over it, adding the odd fleeting highlights to the dark, decaying wood. To capture the dramatic interplay of wood and light properly in the picture, you point the AF metering frame in the centre of the viewfinder first at the wood, leaving the water and sky in the rest of the frame. Store the metered result by pressing the "ML" button, then realign the camera to frame the picture you want and release. You may have captured the right mood, but it is never certain with such dark-on-dark subjects. You would be well advised to try another two or three shots, varying the area metered, say $^1/_3$ to $^2/_3$ lighter to darker sections and then a $^2/_3$ to $^1/_3$ mixture.

This is not a waste of film, but rather a careful and considered reaction to the uncertainties of the metering facility that can only cope perfectly with the average subject. The special result, with the right mood, needs the overriding decision by the photographer, together with a safety margin of several shots to ensure at least one good result.

When shooting in shutter speed priority it is possible to adjust the measured and stored exposure value into various shutter speed/aperture combinations. But this is possible only in this mode!

Contrast compromise step-by-step

Varying the distribution of light and dark in the viewfinder and retaining the appropriate exposure value with the "ML" memory lock button is one possibility for obtaining the correct exposure. The use of the "+/−" correction switch on the left shoulder of the camera is another, and sometimes better way to obtain the same result. For the subject with the white sails and the bright sky you meter the subject exactly with the framing you intend to shoot, and then for each subsequent exposure use compensation factors from +0.5 to +2.0 in half stops. As these compensation factors are always firmly programmed for each shot you can take your time and concentrate on composing the image. The compensation factor will raise or lower the exposure value metered at a particular time, and thus take account of any changes occuring in the meantime. The desired image of the dark wood should then be bracketed with exposure compensations to -2.0. The "+/−" symbol in the viewfinder and the compensation factors displayed in the CENTIC panel remind you that you have applied a compensation and should return it to zero as soon as the series has been taken.

Both methods for influencing the work of the exposure metering system will produce similar results. It is good practice with every film you load in your SFX to try to bracket the exposure for one particular subject to obtain a range of darker and lighter renditions of one particular view. However, when doing this you should also keep an eye on the shutter speed to ensure that your personal camera-shake limit, always considering the focal length of the lens attached, is not exceeded. If the shutter speed blinks in the viewfinder, and the aperture value in the CENTIC display panel, then the exposure control cannot set the required aperture value because it is not available on the lens. In this case the only remedy is to select much faster or slower shutter speeds to get back into the range of available aperture values. The range of subjects where bracketing the exposure could be useful are almost unlimited: landscapes with a large proportion of sky in the viewfinder, portraits against a bright background, strong side lighting, back-lit scenes, subjects in the fog, snowscapes. There is no absolute fixed rule of by how much one should compensate. Some experience will help, but an absolute guarantee is impossible. These experience-based values should be used only as a starting point from which a series of shots with further compensation values should be taken. If we are dealing with a view with an expansive sky, strong side lighting or back-lit shots, the compensation factors should generally be taken to +2.5, for subjects against a light background between +1.5 to +2.5, for subjects against a dark background -1 to -2, and for subjects in the fog or subjects in the snow +1 to +3.

The metering range of the SFX in automatic exposure control covers EV1 (1 second at f/1.4) to EV20 (1/2000 second at f/22) with ISO 100/21° film. The metering characteristic is centre-weighted integrating; which means that the whole frame is metered but the sections at the centre of the frame contribute more strongly to the metering result than the subject details at the edges.

Assigning the Exposure Value

The mixture of metered values of light and shade, and the assignment to a range on the contrast scale, combine subject brightness and film speed as exposure value. This is the definition of the amount of light that the film needs for correct exposure. The means by which the right amount of light is allowed to enter the camera and meet the film is the same for today's high-tech SFX user as it was 50 years ago at the very beginnings of 35mm SLR photography. These functions are performed by the aperture and the focal plane shutter which is immediately in front of the film plane. Both restrict and apportion the amount of light falling on the film in their own particular way. Whether the shutter and aperture are controlled by your fingers or electronically, one premise always applies: a cake may only be divided into two equal parts or into a smaller and a larger portion. The exposure value can be divided likewise. Either you assign half to the shutter speed and half to the aperture value, or you allow a slower shutter speed, which means the aperture has to be stopped down, or the aperture is opened up and the shutter speeded up accordingly. Whatever the type or method of dividing the exposure value, it is bound by the measured light quantity and cannot be increased or decreased unless you deliberately wish to over- or underexpose the film.

The focal plane shutter

In this Pentax model the shutter travels immediately in front of the film from bottom to top. The first blind consists of five extremely fine blades of exceedingly hard man-made material; the second blind is constructed from four similar blades and two metal blades. These extremely light blades reach their full speed of travel practically from the moment they leave their rest position. The exposure time or shutter speed is formed by the fixed speed of the blinds and the width of the slit they form when traversing the film plane. It is therefore the width of the slit that determines the shutter speed. This is set either automatically by the exposure control of the SFX, or, in shutter speed priority or manual modes, by the photographer via the select switch next to the release button. The first shutter blind is started by the microprocessor of the SFX only after the

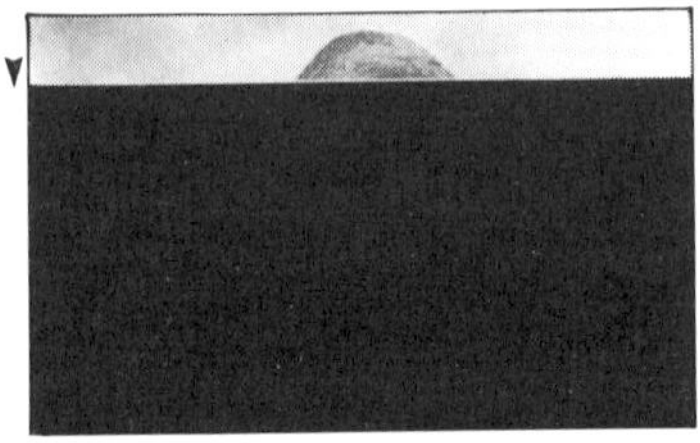

As soon as the shutter release is activated, the first shutter blind starts its journey across the film plane and the first part of the film is exposed.

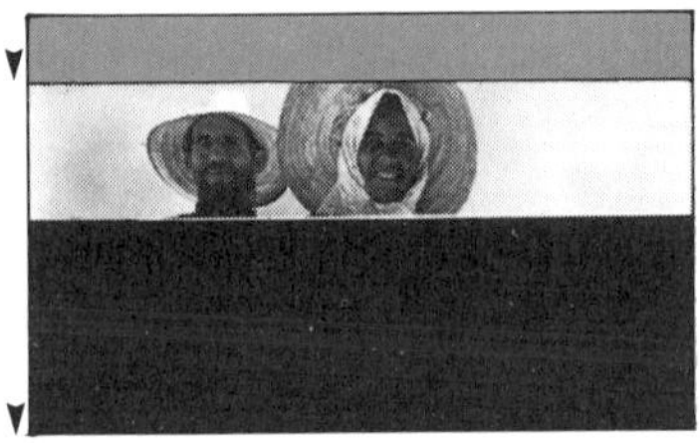

If the selected shutter speed is faster than $^{1}/_{100}$ second, then the second blind starts before the first has reached the other side.

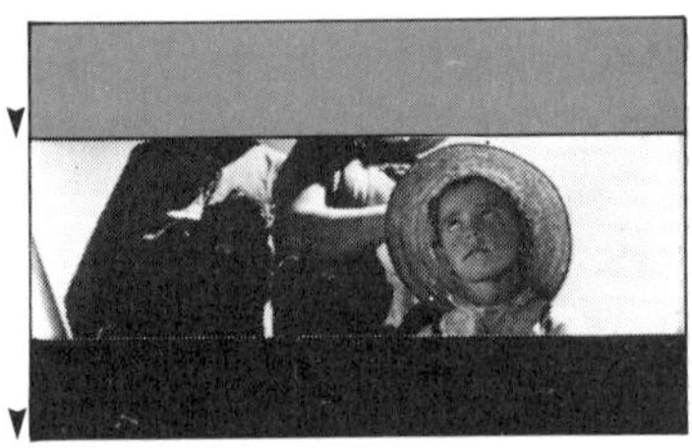

Both shutter blinds move across the film plane. The size of the slit decreases as the set shutter speed becomes faster.

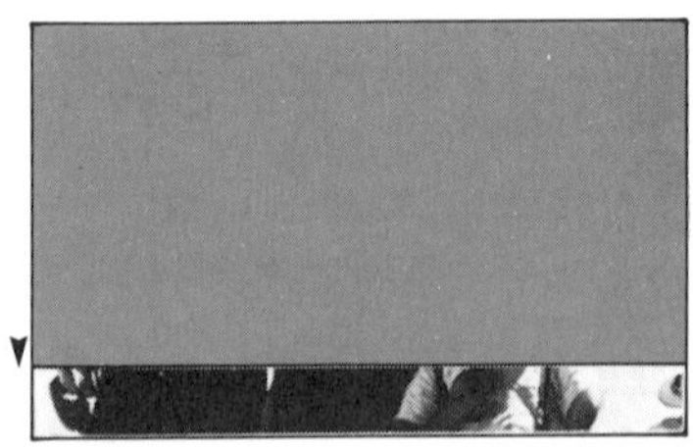

The second blind completes the exposure process. The total shutter travelling time is longer than the exposure time.

The shutter is cocked for the next exposure. The shutter blinds are returned to their initial position.

exposure metering and automatic focusing has been completed. The second shutter blind follows to close the film gate after the time calculated by the computer. The automatic shutter control can set infinitely variable shutter speeds from $^1/_{2000}$ to 30 seconds. The manually selectable shutter speeds lie on the well-known scale of values from $^1/_{2000}$ to 1 second. There is also $^1/_{100}$ second as the synchronization time for non-system flashguns and "bulb" for long exposures, which requires the use of Cable Switch F.

In automatic shooting modes the shutter speeds from $^1/_{2000}$ to 30 seconds are displayed in the CENTIC panel. In the viewfinder the display of actual times ends with "2", the display for $^1/_2$ second, all longer times are indicated as "LT". As a consequence of the structure of a focal plane (slit) shutter, the actual travelling time of the shutter blinds across the film gate is always longer than the effective shutter speed, and always longer than the flash illumination time of electronic flash. The flash can fully illuminate the film format only if the slit between the two shutter blinds is wider than 24mm, which is the width of the narrower side of the film. This means the second blind has to start after the first has reached the other side and the whole frame is exposed for at least a few milliseconds. This is the case at $^1/_{100}$ second and for all longer times in the case of the SFX. If a Pentax AF flashgun is attached, the flash synchronization speed is set automatically.

The duty, functioning and effect of the focal plane shutter of the SFX is quite easy to understand. A shutter speed of $^1/_{250}$ second allows twice as much light through as a speed of $^1/_{500}$ second, but only half as much light as $^1/_{125}$ second.

This is not the only duty that the shutter performs. It also offers a choice of fast shutter speeds to capture a moving subject as a sharp image and freeze its movement. No shutter speed is too fast for anything moving faster than a cyclist. On the other hand, the speed-blurred limbs of an athlete, the twirling legs of a dancer, the blurred contours of a motor-cross rider create an image that is dynamic, a quality missing from the frozen, yet sharp image of the moment of movement.

The shutter is also used to keep the camera-shake devil at bay. One general rule applies here as with any other camera. The inverse of the shutter speed in seconds should be no less than the focal length in mm of the lens attached. In other words, for a 50mm lens the limit for shake-free shooting is generally taken to be $^1/_{60}$ second. The shutter speeds for the AF 300mm, f/3.5 ED/IF lens should start with values faster than $^1/_{250}$ second, and if the 70-210mm, f/4-5.6 AF-Zoom is used, the speed should be about the same.

The aperture

Take the AF 50mm, f/1.4 lens, turn the aperture ring to f/1.4 and back and observe the opening formed by the eight delicate blades. These form the varying sized openings that control the amount of light allowed through to the film. The larger the hole, the more light is allowed to enter. The aperture does not control the light by time, as the shutter does, but by the diameter of the opening in relation to the focal length of the lens.

The area of the circle is quadrupled if the diameter is doubled. The diameter multiplied by the factor $\sqrt{2}$ (= 1.414) doubles the circular area and therefore the amount of light entering. Reducing the diameter by dividing it by 1.414 halves the area and thus the amount of light by half. The light-regulating effect of the aperture size depends also on the distance to the film, i.e. the focal length of the lens. In order to be able to compare the optically-effective size of the aperture in lenses with various focal lengths, opticians state the diameter of the aperture not in actual mm, but as the focal length divided by the diameter of the aperture circle. This value is called the aperture value, or f/number. It is the f/number that we employ directly in assessing the calculated

---

White blooms in front of a large dark background are always effective. Usually a compensation of -0.5 to -1 will be needed. This may be taken in aperture priority, shutter speed priority or program mode, AF 35-135mm Zoom.

Photo: Richard Hünecke

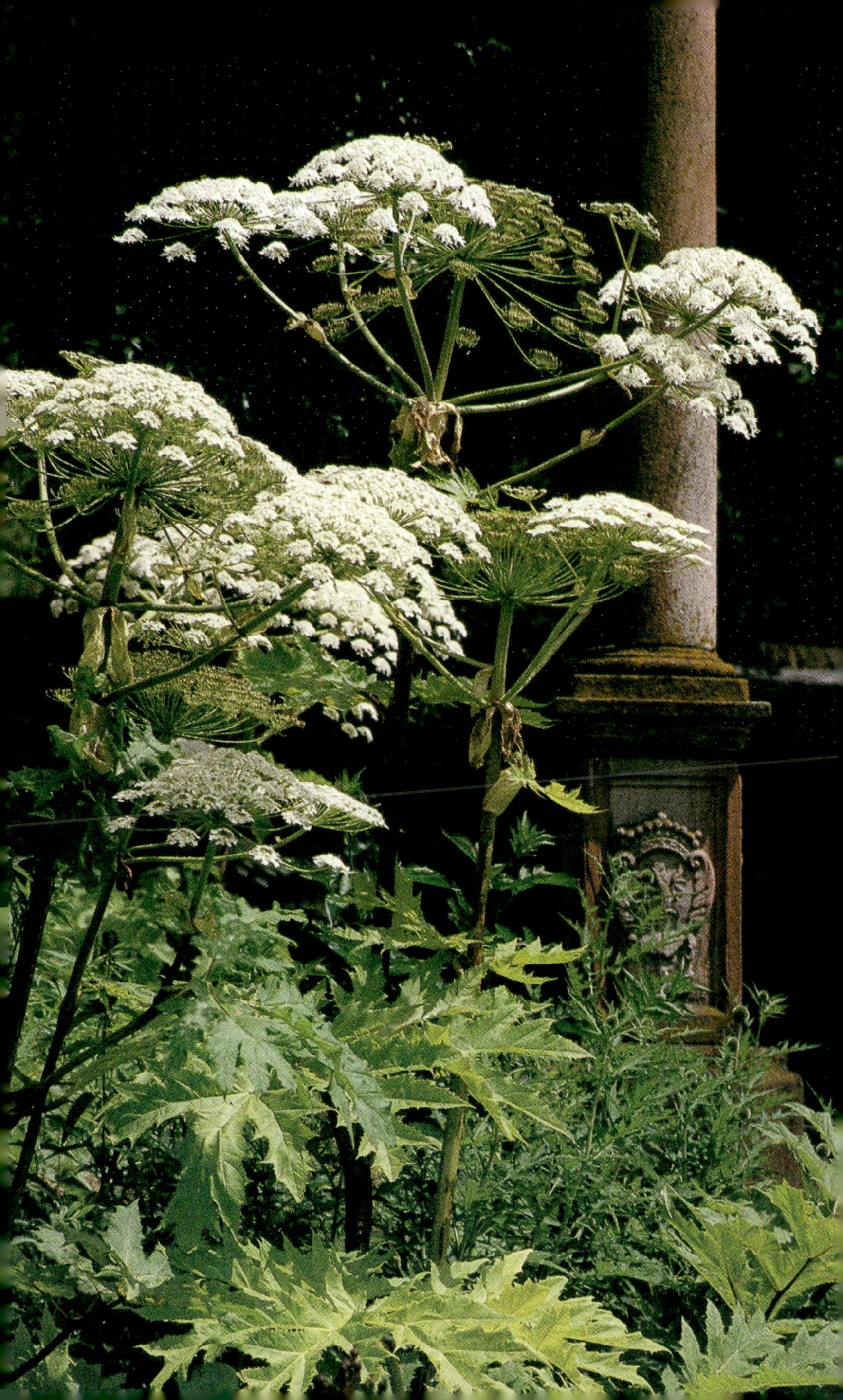

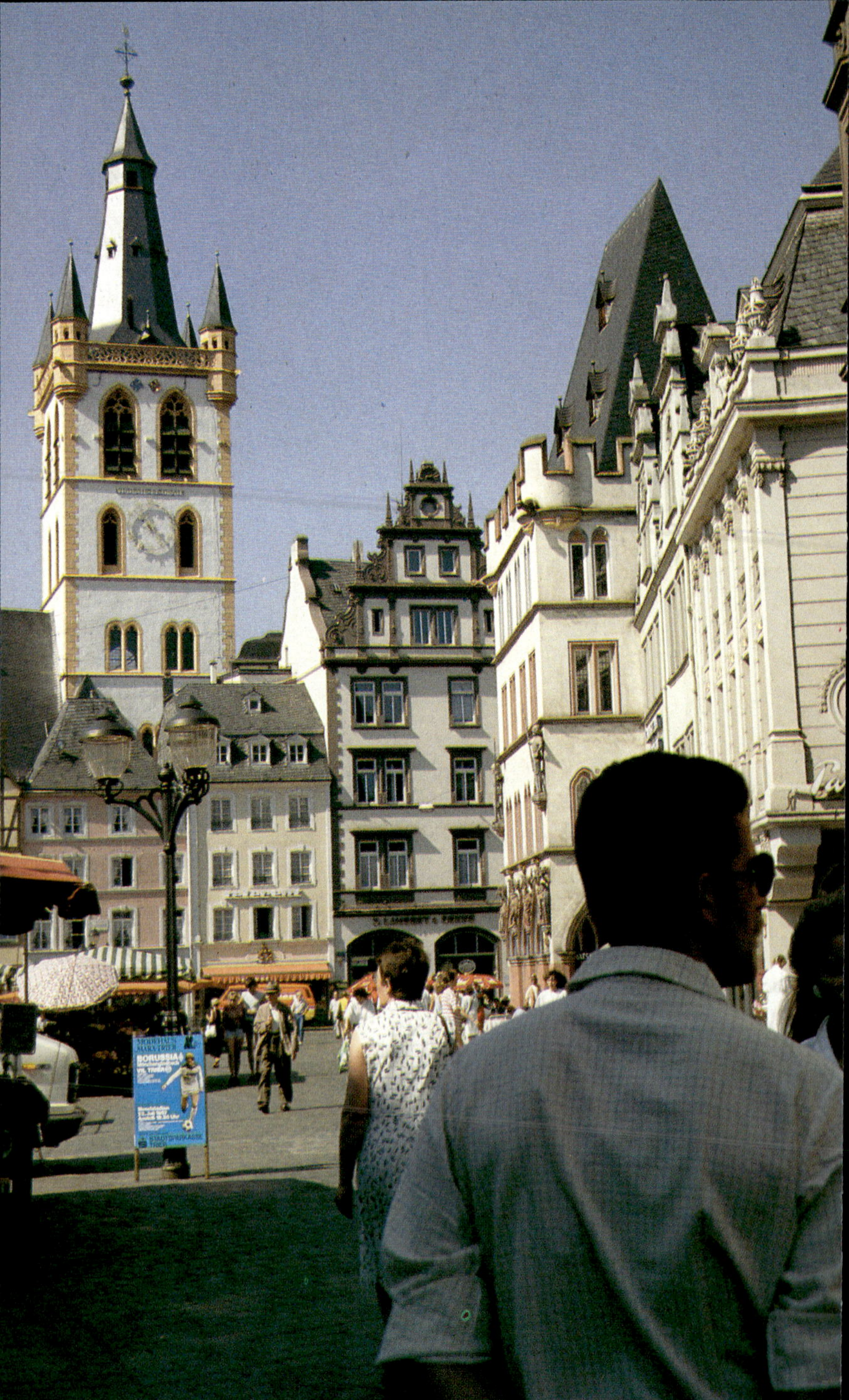
BORUSSIA

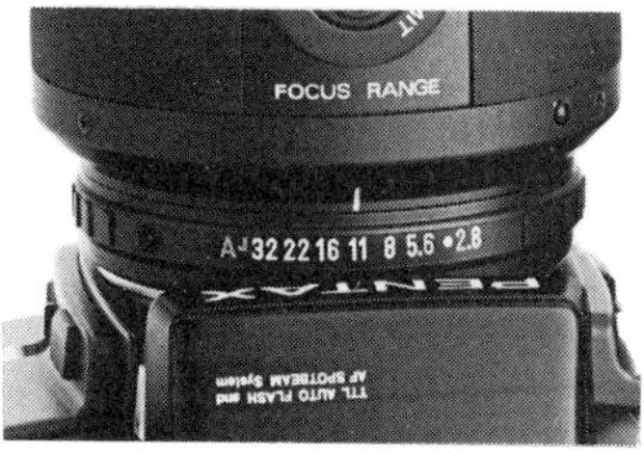

The size of the aperture is determined by the aperture ring – here the Pentax AF 100,f/2.8 Macro lens.

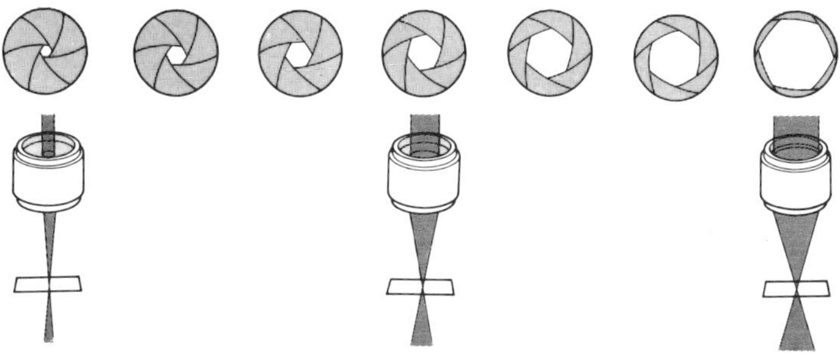

The opening formed by the aperture leaves determines the amount of light allowed to pass through the lens.

exposure value in terms of aperture value and shutter speed.

Aperture f/1.4, or f/4, or f/11, or f/16 means for all lenses of any focal length that the optically effective diameter of these apertures is $^{1}/_{1.4}$, or $^{1}/_{4}$, or $^{1}/_{11}$ or $^{1}/_{16}$ respectively of the focal length of the lens. From this sequence we derive the series of f/numbers. These are displayed in the CENTIC panel for the program and shutter speed priority modes of the SFX. The smallest number is always the largest aperture opening, the largest number always the smallest. Changing the aperture value by one stop, in increasing or decreasing order, allows half

---

Shafts of sunlight add interest to the facades of the buildings, but it throws the foreground into deep shadow. I tried a few exposure compensation settings to +1.5 to obtain the best compromise. If you want to obtain small exposure compensations then the ISO film speed setting is the best method. Each ISO setting corresponds to a $^{1}/_{3}$ f-stop correction. This view was taken with the AF 24-50mm Zoom. *Photo: Richard Hünecke*

as much or double the amount of light through. This is one of the key principles of photography. The f/stop sequence runs as follows: f/1, f/1.4, f/2, f/2.8, f/4, f/5.6, f/8, f/11, f/16, f/22, f/32, f/45, f/64...

Always depending on aperture value and initial lens speed, Pentax AF lenses also have intermediate half-stops available up to f/11 or f/16.

Remarks on depth of field

The aperture has another effect on the photographic process. If it is closed to a small opening, then the rays of light allowed through will be narrow and pointed. Even the best quality lenses gain reproduction quality if they are stopped down by one or two stops. This narrow beam is the reason why the depth of field is greatest with small apertures. The depth of field is the distance from the nearest to the furthest planes in the subject that are represented sharply on the film, covering some distance in front and some behind the plane of focus. One should say "appears to be sharp" because a point in the image is only a sharp point on the film if it was at the plane of focus. Away from the plane of focus it will be spread into a disc, called the circle of confusion, which is bigger the further the point is from the plane of focus. Because below a certain size the human eye is unable to distinguish between a point and a circle, we may think a feature in the subject is in focus when it is not. This is the basis of depth of field – it is an optical illusion. For photographic purposes the limits of depth of field are defined as when the circle of confusion becomes greater than 0.033mm in diameter. If the aperture is stopped down, the depth of field is increased, opening the aperture decreases the depth of field. The depth of field is always shallower in the close-up range than for more distant settings up to infinity. A lens with a longer focal length produces, at each aperture/distance combination, a shallower depth of field than one with a shorter focal length.

The degree of subsequent enlargement of a slide or negative, and the viewing distance to the screen or print are also decisive factors in the choice of correct aperture. If you are quite happy with 10x15cm (4x6in) prints, or never project your slides any wider than 75cm (30in), then you can always choose an aperture one stop larger than suggested in the Depth of Field tables at the back of the book. In this case the slides ought to be viewed at a distance of at least 1m (40in). If, however, you go for poster-size prints or like to project your slides to a width of 180cm (6ft), also allowing that you might view them from about 80cm (30in) distance, then you should not use the aperture stated in the table. If, say, f/5.6 was suggested, use the next smaller aperture f/8 to obtain extra depth of field. The circles of confusion increase at the same rate as the negative is enlarged on a print or slide on the screen.

Depth of field therefore is not a fixed parameter such as focal length or guide number. It is an interesting and effective means of image creation. The smaller aperture openings of a wide-angle lens will render everything in the picture from close-up to infinity uniformly sharp. The larger apertures of the fast telephoto AF 300mm, f/4.5 ED/IF – for this focal length this is considered fast – manages in the close range only a few centimetres of depth of field and in the medium range perhaps a few metres. But wait until you also add to this the streaks of light from the sun low on the horizon and you will have taken another step towards individual and creative picture making. However, an extremely narrow depth of field with the main subject very sharp and with the background floating into an undefined coloured haze is not to everyone's taste. On the other hand, some photographers use this technique with feeling and great skill.

The way the aperture brings depth of field into the picture cannot be appreciated on the focusing screen. The Pentax SFX has no stop-down lever. Did the Asahi engineers simply forget it? Well, it is true that stopping down the aperture makes the viewfinder image increasingly darker and with each stop it gets more difficult to assess the depth of field. Moreover, the stop-down lever makes little sense when using the program mode. To allow the program mode freedom to use all available aperture/shutter speed combinations it has to be able to set the aperture freely. Using the stop down lever it would be set to the smallest aperture and then it would be difficult to assess the image. But in aperture priority, where the aperture is selected manually, and in metered manual mode the provision of a stop-down lever would have been useful.

Choice of Exposure Mode

Aperture and shutter, being interconnected and obeying the strict prescription of exposure value, control the amount of light reaching the film. If one of the pair allows a lot of light through, the other has to come into play and cut it short. Whether the exposure value is divided according to the program mode of the SFX, or if you decide which proportion is assigned to each by turning aperture ring and shutter speed dial on your old manual camera, it does not matter. As long as the basic rules are followed the film will be correctly exposed. An automatic camera only does it faster, reliably and with greater precision.

The Pentax SFX offers the biggest range of modes you could possibly want: full program, shutter speed priority, aperture priority, and manual modes. These may be divided into two groups. For one group – shutter speed priority with preselected shutter speed and program mode with its five variations – you set the aperture ring to "A". For the other group you turn the aperture ring to a particular f/number and you can then shoot either in aperture priority mode or in manual mode. You also select the shutter speed in the latter case. Changing the lens does not necessitate re-programming the selected shooting mode. The programmed flash mode is a special case and will be dealt with in detail later.

Shutter speed priority

Proceed as follows: turn the aperture ring to "A", slide the MODE switch forward and operate the select switch until

AUTO is displayed on the top line of the CENTIC display panel. The shutter speed is then chosen by operating the select switch again and this information is displayed on the left of the centre line of the CENTIC panel. After the release has been pressed lightly the automatically-selected aperture value will be displayed on the right of the centre line next to the letter "F". After fully pressing the release button the shutter speed and "A" are displayed on the right-hand panel of the viewfinder. If you need to know the automatically selected aperture value after checking the subject in the viewfinder, you have to press the "ML" button to keep the metered values stored, then take your eye from the viewfinder and check the information in the CENTIC panel.

Usually you select shutter speed priority because you need to use a fast shutter speed to catch a fast-moving subject sharply. Even if you follow a footballer who has just moved from a sunlit to a shady part of the pitch, the shutter speed will remain fast, only the aperture will follow the changing lighting conditions and open up. This is no problem for the SFX, even with wide open aperture the autofocus will ensure that you get a sharp shot. And as the term suggests, the aperture value plays second fiddle in the shutter speed priority mode.

Shutter speed priority is the ideal tool for sports, games, and any fast action, also for use with long lenses and hand-held close-ups. Generally speaking this is my favourite shooting mode and I change to aperture priority only if I am dealing with a subject where the depth of field needs to be controlled. But

If the aperture ring on the lens is set to A, then AUTO in the CENTIC display panel means shutter speed priority. The arrow pointing at the number 250 means that you have to preselect the shutter speed in this mode. The automatically-selected aperture value appears in the display panel only after the release is depressed. The lower line gives information on shooting frequency, here single frame, and that the first frame is ready to be exposed.

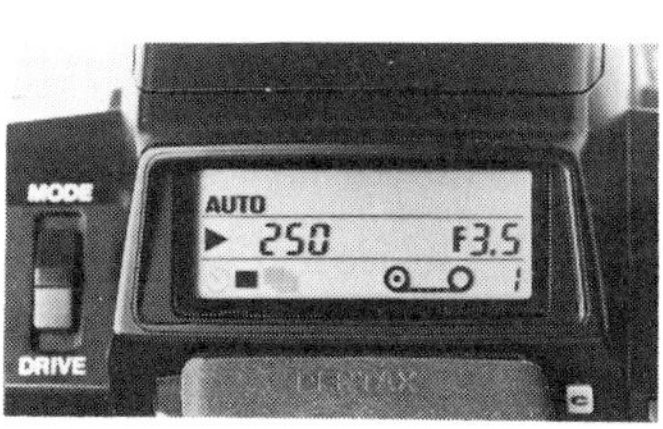

what is a suitable shutter speed? The first consideration is camera-shake. As mentioned previously, for a 50mm lens the shutter speed should not be less than 1/60 second, for the AF 300mm, f/4.5 or the longest focal length on the AF zoom 70-210mm the slowest time is 1/250 second, but I would suggest that 1/500 second is by far a much safer speed. If you are able to support the camera or your arm on a solid support, then you might risk a slightly slower speed. But the movement of the subject itself will dictate the shutter speed. If you wish to freeze your youngster on his bike at 10m distance, then you need about 1/250 second. If you pan the camera with the movement of the bike you should be right with 1/125 second. For all other subjects that move faster than a bike 1/500 second may be considered the standard speed. At this speed the aperture should still have a little scope. It could happen, though, that in subdued afternoon light "500" blinks rapidly in the viewfinder. This means that the exposure control cannot set the required large aperture setting as it does not exist on your lens. In this case you have to change to a slower speed, even if this brings you dangerously close to your personal camera-shake zone. On the other hand a picture with slightly speed-blurred legs and circular speed lines instead of spokes will have a dynamic impact. Another way out is to use a faster lens, if one is handy at the time.

Aperture priority

Procedure: move the aperture ring from the "A" position to the required aperture value, to obtain the required depth of field for

If the aperture ring on the lens is moved from the A position to a number, then AUTO in the CENTIC panel means aperture priority. The arrow pointing at F means you have to preselect the appropriate aperture value. The automatically-calculated shutter speed will be displayed after the release had been lightly pressed.

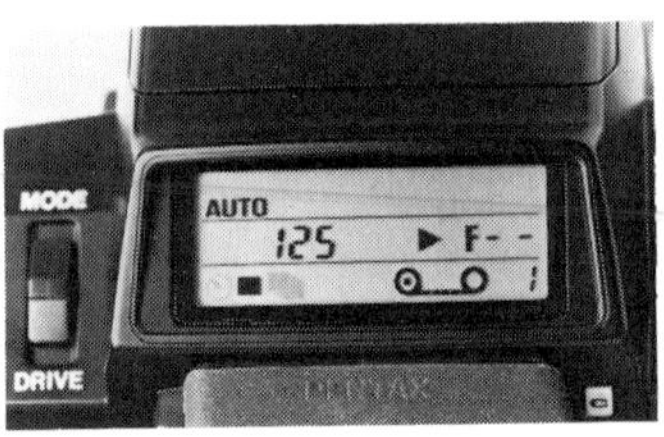

the subject in question. Use the MODE-key to select AUTO to be displayed in the top line of the CENTIC panel.

Information: the index arrow in the second row of the CENTIC panel moves to the right to point at "F", indicating that the aperture value is now the parameter that has to be preselected. When the release is pressed lightly the appropriate shutter speed, metered and calculated by the microprocessor, appears to the left of the aperture value. The shutter speed is also displayed in the viewfinder beneath the "A". The aperture value is not displayed in the viewfinder, because the protruding cap of the SFX has no window for it. But this is no more than a minor inconvenience because you will always want to select the most suitable aperture value for every subject in this shooting mode. The aperture priority mode comes into its own when dealing with subjects where the depth of field is important for a particular subject in the picture. For example, there is the landscape that requires absolute sharpness from the closest detail to the far-away mountains, or the architectural photograph which also requires absolute sharpness of every little detail, or the critical depth of field in close-up and macro photography. A limited depth of field on the other hand is used to good effect in portraits, where you restrict the depth of field to the face, focusing on the eyes, allowing surrounding details to blend into a pleasant but undefined backdrop. A fully open aperture is a powerful tool in creating effective images by limiting the sharply-focused planes and differentiating the important from the incidental.

If we consider just the middle aperture range we soon recognize that we humans have no natural instinct for appreciating what effect aperture values f/4, f/8 or f/16 have on the final picture. Moreover, depth of field does not diminish suddenly, but declines gradually. In a 10x15cm print this presents no problem, but if it is enlarged to 30x45cm, then the gradation into unsharpness is clearly discernible. How does the cautious photographer deal with this situation? He stops down two stops more than would be absolutely necessary in favour of greater depth of field. This will often lead into dangerously slow shutter speeds that only the brave or the foolhardy attempts unaided. The exposure computer in the SFX will permit the entire range of shutter speeds from $^1/_{2000}$ to 30 seconds. If "2000" or "LT" are flashing in the viewfinder, then this range is insufficient; you have to select a smaller or larger aperture to get within metering range. These typical reactions represent for me the weakness of aperture priority mode. In strong and rapidly-changing lighting conditions the shutter speed could easily drop below the hand-held limit and, despite the clear information panel in the viewfinder, this may be easily overlooked if the action in front of the camera holds your complete attention. Then, although the less important depth of field remains constant, because the aperture is preselected the shutter speed is out of bounds.

Program mode

Procedure: set the aperture ring to "A" and activate the MODE button and select switch until PROGRAM and the symbol for one of the program variations are displayed in the CENTIC panel. Alternatively, press the "C" button.

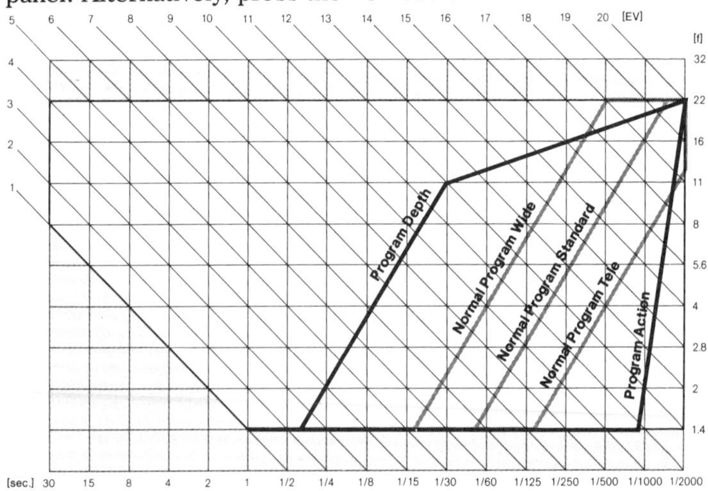

Diagram of shutter speed/aperture values in the individual variations of program mode.

Information: when the release is pressed, the shutter speed and aperture value are displayed in the centre line of the CENTIC display panel. Both of these values are the ones that the program mode will have selected automatically in keeping with the particular program variation chosen. In the viewfinder of the SFX you will see only the shutter speed beneath the "P". If you want to check the aperture value when you have decided on the framing of the subject, then you have to press the "ML" button with your thumb and refer to the CENTIC panel.

Shutter speeds and aperture values are so graduated that the next lower or higher value allowed to expose the film doubles or halves the amount of light. A change in shutter speed from $^1/_{60}$ to $^1/_{500}$ second will open the aperture from f/11 to f/4 and the exposure value remains unchanged – a shutter speed of $^1/_{60}$ at f/11 is equivalent to $^1/_{500}$ at f/4, both corresponding to EV13. Following this step along the EV-line you obtain safe shutter speeds with long lenses, short times for sports photography, and also a narrower depth of field suitable for many subjects. One of the secrets of successful photography is this movement along the EV-line and making a correct choice of shutter speed/aperture combination to give the best compromise between shutter speed and depth of field to record the subject in the way you want.

Every exposure value may be divided into several equivalent combinations of shutter speed and f/number. The exposure computer in the SFX processes the metered values and the programmed data into electronic signals which are translated by the control functions into the movements of the shutter blinds and the diaphragm blades. Consequently there is no problem in obtaining from every metered exposure value the suitable combination and translating this into a photographically average situation, which is then assigned to a program curve. Exposure value 1, corresponding to the lower working limit of the SFX, corresponds to 1 second at f/1.4, or 30 seconds at f/8. The aperture priority mode is capable of setting both of these combinations. Exposure value 20, the upper limit, corresponds to $^1/_{2000}$ second at f/22 or $^1/_{500}$ second at f/45. If we connect these limit value pairs by a straight line obliquely through all exposure value lines, then the resultant program curve would be theoretically feasible, but it would not have any practical value.

The normal program

This is indicated by NORMAL beneath an empty square frame in the top line of the CENTIC display panel. There are three variations, these are automatically selected by the SFX in accordance with the focal length lens is attached to the camera.

The ***Standard Variation*** applies for all focal lengths between 40mm and 110mm, and is also employed for exposure control if a wide-angle or a telephoto zoom lens is used within this range. A symbol of two stylized trees appears in the square frame on the top line of the the display panel indicating this variation. This program curve intersects the lines for EV8 at $^{1}/_{70}$ second and f/1.8 and for EV10 at $^{1}/_{125}$ second at f/2.8. EV12 intersects the curve at $^{1}/_{190}$ second and f/4.5 and EV14 at $^{1}/_{350}$ second at f/6.7. Down to $^{1}/_{50}$ second the curve remains at f/1.4 and f/22 is reached at about $^{1}/_{1500}$ second. This means that in this program mode faster shutter speeds are preferred rather than smaller aperture openings. If a slower lens is used, then the standard program is forced to control the exposure by reducing the shutter speed with the aperture fully open. The relatively steep slope of the standard program curve takes us fairly quickly to exposure times faster than $^{1}/_{125}$ second, even if the lighting conditions are not very bright. This is desirable

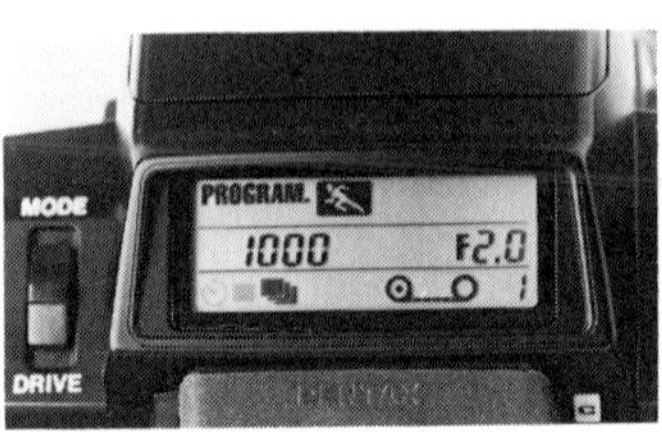

The standard program of the SFX is displayed in the CENTIC panel by PROGRAM and NORMAL; the program variation for the focal length in use is indicated by the two-tree symbol in the NORMAL frame for focal lengths between 40 and 110mm. Shutter speed and aperture values are displayed only after the release button has been pressed.

for enjoying the facilities offered by the AF 100mm, f/2.8 Macro lens.

The ***Telephoto Variation*** is automatically selected if the focal length of the lens attached (or the zoom setting) exceeds 110mm. The choice of this variation is indicated by a single tree in the square frame on the top line of the panel. The TELE curve starts theoretically at about 1/150 second and f/1.4. However, speeds of f/1.4 for lenses in excess of 110mm are still wishful thinking. Reality starts at the more down-to-earth f/4 for the AF 70-210mm Zoom, although the AF 135mm, f/2.8 should be available by the time this book is in print. At f/4 a shutter speed of 1/500 second is prescribed, which corresponds to EV13. If the lighting conditions fall below this level then the program curve is forced to reduce the shutter speed down to 1 second. The TELE-curve responds to better lighting conditions, starting with 1/500 second and f/4 and continuing in a straight line to 1/2000 second at f/11. From this point only the aperture may be stopped down to the smallest opening. This curve is governed by the necessity to always select fast enough shutter speeds to accommodate the longer focal lengths.

The ***Wide-angle Variation*** of the standard program applies automatically for focal lengths of 40mm and less. The CENTIC display will indicate this by three stylized trees in the square above the word NORMAL. In the diagram the WIDE curve starts with 1/20 second at f/1.4. However, at present the Pentax range does not include a wide-angle lens of this speed so the WIDE program starts at f/3.5, the largest available aperture opening, with a corresponding shutter speed of 1/45 second. For poorer lighting conditions only the shutter speed can be reduced. For better lighting conditions the program curve rises from 1/90 second at f/5.6 and 1/250 second at f/11, from then the shutter speeds can be increased to 1/2000 second. The average exposure value of EV13 is assigned as 1/125 second at f/8 – a combination that is suitable for a wide variety of situations. f/8 produces a large depth of field and with focal lengths below 40mm 1/125 second is absolutely safe. The

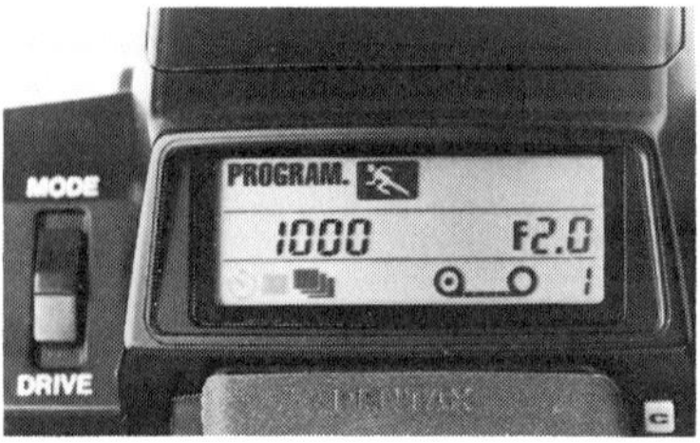

The sprinting figure next to PROGRAM indicates the ACTION program variation which favours fast shutter speeds as against wide apertures. This mode is often useful with the continuous shooting mode, indicated by the fan symbol.

AF 28mm, f/2.8 should also be available and this program variable will select $^{1}/_{45}$ second for the fully open aperture – still quite a safe and useful combination.

The automatic program variations of the Pentax SFX are not infallible under all circumstances. This may be demonstrated by turning the AF 35-135mm, f/3.5 Zoom from the longest to the shortest focal length and observing what happens. As intended, the program variation changes from TELE to STANDARD to WIDE and for EV12 assigns first $^{1}/_{250}$ second at f/4, then $^{1}/_{180}$ second at f/4.5, and finally $^{1}/_{90}$ second at f/6.7. For the 135mm setting the $^{1}/_{250}$ second is quite correct and would be suitable for instance to capture the cyclists racing towards you. The shot presented to you only a few seconds later, when the riders are sprinting past, would have been a lovely one if the shutter speed of $^{1}/_{90}$ second, selected by the wide-angle variation of the standard program, had not been too slow to produce a really sharp image of the mounted horde, but too fast for a speed-blurred impression of the mad scramble. The wide depth of field reaching to infinity, produced by an aperture of f/6.7, would not save it from the wastepaper basket either. After all, we usually put a wide-angle lens on the camera, or turn the zoom to its shortest focal length, because we want to accommodate a large subject area in the frame, and also because we want to distinguish between foreground and background by the extreme differentiation in size which gives the image a special atmosphere; not because we need the very wide depth of field! With a focal length of 35mm, $^{1}/_{250}$ second is obtained only from f/11, and this corresponds to an exposure value of 15. If you were using an ISO 100/21° film this EV value would correspond to a very bright sunny day. The only other way to obtain this shutter speed in program mode would be to reload with an ISO 800/30° film.

To handle the bicycle race I would turn to shutter speed priority mode, preselect 1/250 second, and let the exposure control decide on the correct aperture.

Two special programs for special subjects

The Pentax SFX has no program shift; instead it has two program variations – "Speed Depth Program" and "Special Action Program". These differ from the NORMAL program mode in that they give you more predictable combinations, with the bias towards fast shutter speeds or small apertures, regardless of what focal length lens is attached as long as it has a K-, KA- or KAF- bayonet. The ***Special Action Program***, indicated by the sprinting figure in the top line of the CENTIC display and activated by the MODE button and Select switch as usual, is more or less a special form of shutter speed priority. Depending on lens speed, the aperture will be kept open to obtain shutter speeds of around 1/1000 second. The speeds and aperture values are changed only within the relatively small range of 1/2000 to 1/1000 second, following a steep program curve in this range. In this program mode, more often than not, you will shoot with the aperture wide open. If the resulting narrow depth of field is not detrimental – it may even be desirable – you will be very well served by this mode for those fast action shots, and always be assured that the shutter speed is fast enough to avoid the effects of camera shake.

Pushing the MODE switch and sliding the select switch twice takes you to the ***Special Depth Program***, which is symbolized by the pictograph of a man and a mountain in the square. This program curve starts with f/1.4 and 1/3 second because it can be used with any focal length lens. f/4 in this program mode is attained at 1/8 second and f/11 is combined with 1/30 second. From this point the curve follows a clearly flatter gradient; there are only two aperture stops, f/16 and f/22, to be combined with the remaining shutter speeds to

$^1/_{2000}$ second. One thing is clear: shooting in the DEPTH mode requires good light to obtain reasonably fast shutter speeds, otherwise a tripod would be needed or a fairly fast film. The difference between the Special Depth Program and manual preselection in aperture priority mode is that in the latter you select the aperture value according to your requirements, in Special Depth Program, the camera computer will do it for you.

In both these program modes the aperture value and shutter speed will be displayed in the CENTIC panel. In the viewfinder only the shutter speed is seen beneath the "P".

I should like to emphasise again that when a lens is changed nothing will be cancelled or changed in the selected exposure program.

Manual setting of aperture and shutter speed

Now we come to the manual selection of aperture and shutter speed in metered manual mode. Turn the aperture ring from "A" and set it to a value suitable for the subject. Operate the MODE switch and the select switch until MAN is displayed in the CENTIC panel.

Information: in the centre line of the CENTIC panel only the shutter speed will be displayed, next to "F" are two bars "– –", the aperture is set on the aperture ring and so the value is not displayed. In the viewfinder "M" will light up to indicate manual mode, together with two shutter speeds. One shutter speed will be flashing; this is the one that the exposure control has calculated from the subject brightness and selected aperture. The other is constantly alight, this is the value that you have selected. For correct exposure you have to either adjust the aperture or change the shutter speed by the select switch, or a combination of both, until the two shutter speed displays combine to one single, constantly-lit value. The manually selectable shutter speeds range from $^1/_{2000}$ to 1 second. In order to make fine adjustments it would have been convenient to have the aperture value displayed in the viewfinder.

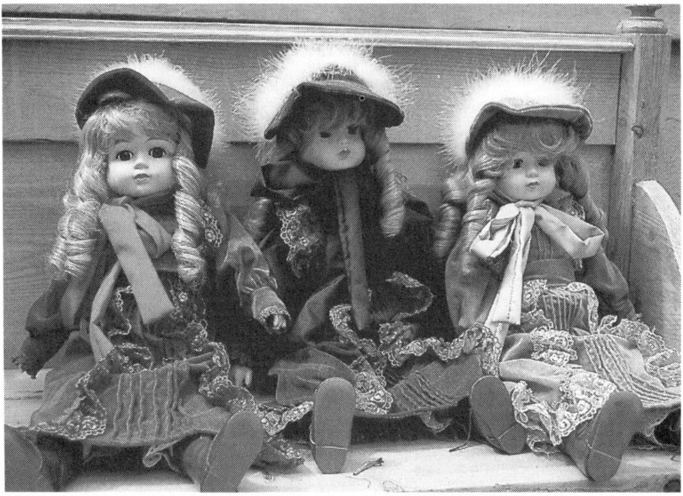

Regardless of whether your portrait subjects are real people or dolls, the point to focus on is always the eyes of the model. The above shot was taken with the AF f/1.4,50mm lens.

But what aperture value should you preselect, by how much should you adjust this value to obtain the correct exposure value? These questions are subject to the same considerations as aperture selection in aperture priority mode, or shutter speed selection in shutter speed priority mode. If the depth of field is the overriding parameter, you select the aperture and the shutter speed has to follow. If the subject is lively and you want to catch it in its transient state, you adjust the aperture to suit the shutter speed. And what are the situations where you would select manual mode, rather than one of the other automatic modes? Scenes where aperture and shutter speed have to be kept constant because a varying light and dark background could intrude in the narrow metering field of the SFX and influence the automatic exposure control to an unwanted and undesirable degree. This could be the case in indoor sports activities, for example. The lighting in the arena does not change, but the subjects move swiftly, athletes dressed in dark or light colours move in and out of your frame,

MAN and arrows pointing to both the shutter speed and the F in the CENTIC panel indicate metered manual mode. The continuous shooting mode is in no way unsuitable.

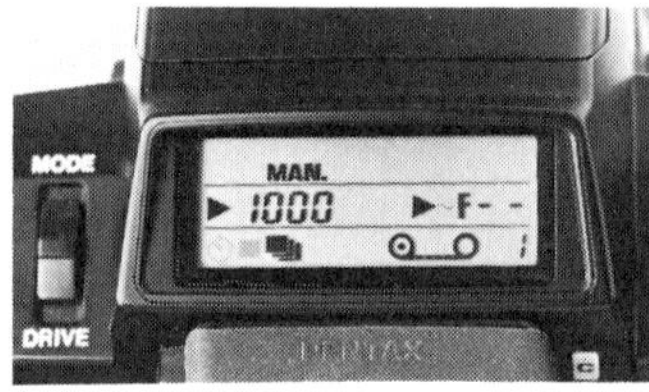

which itself sometimes covers a greater proportion of the brightly polished floor, sometimes more of the dark panelling on the sides. As long as you are covering the activities at the centre of the arena, you maintain the same exposure value. As soon as you take some pictures of the spectators, you take the exposure based on a new measurement. The same applies to a portrait series with changing backgrounds. As long as the shooting direction is not changed, or only slightly, you retain the same aperture/shutter speed combination: you only need to concentrate on catching the right pose, the pleasant expression, and the camera will do the rest, including focusing.

The autofocus system in the SFX reacts very fast, but this shot of the rapid descent of the toboggan down the track would not have been possible in AF mode. The old trick used by many sports photographers is useful for situations such as this: focus on a point on the track and release the instant the driver passes through it. AF 70-210mm Zoom. Photo: Richard Hünecke

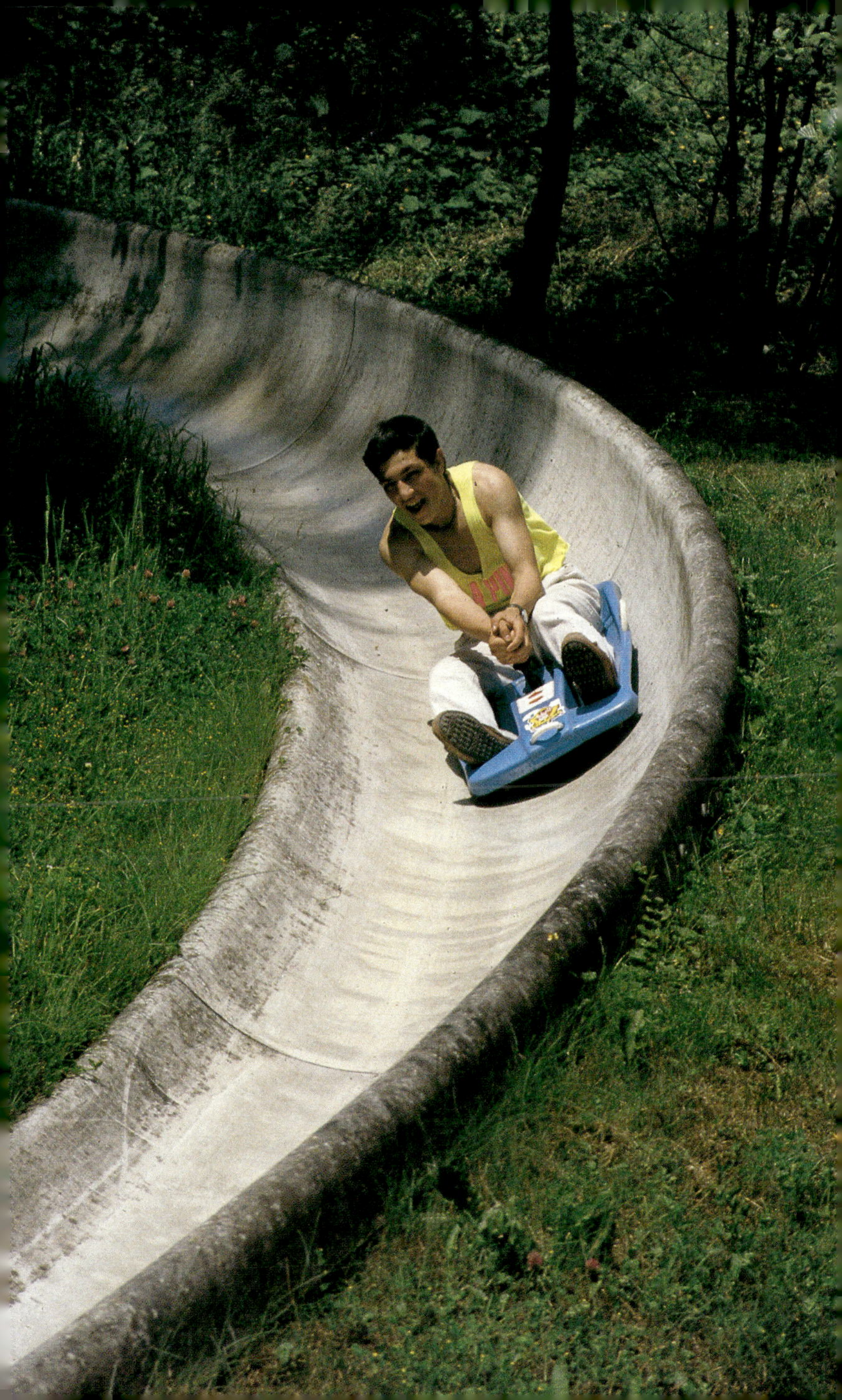

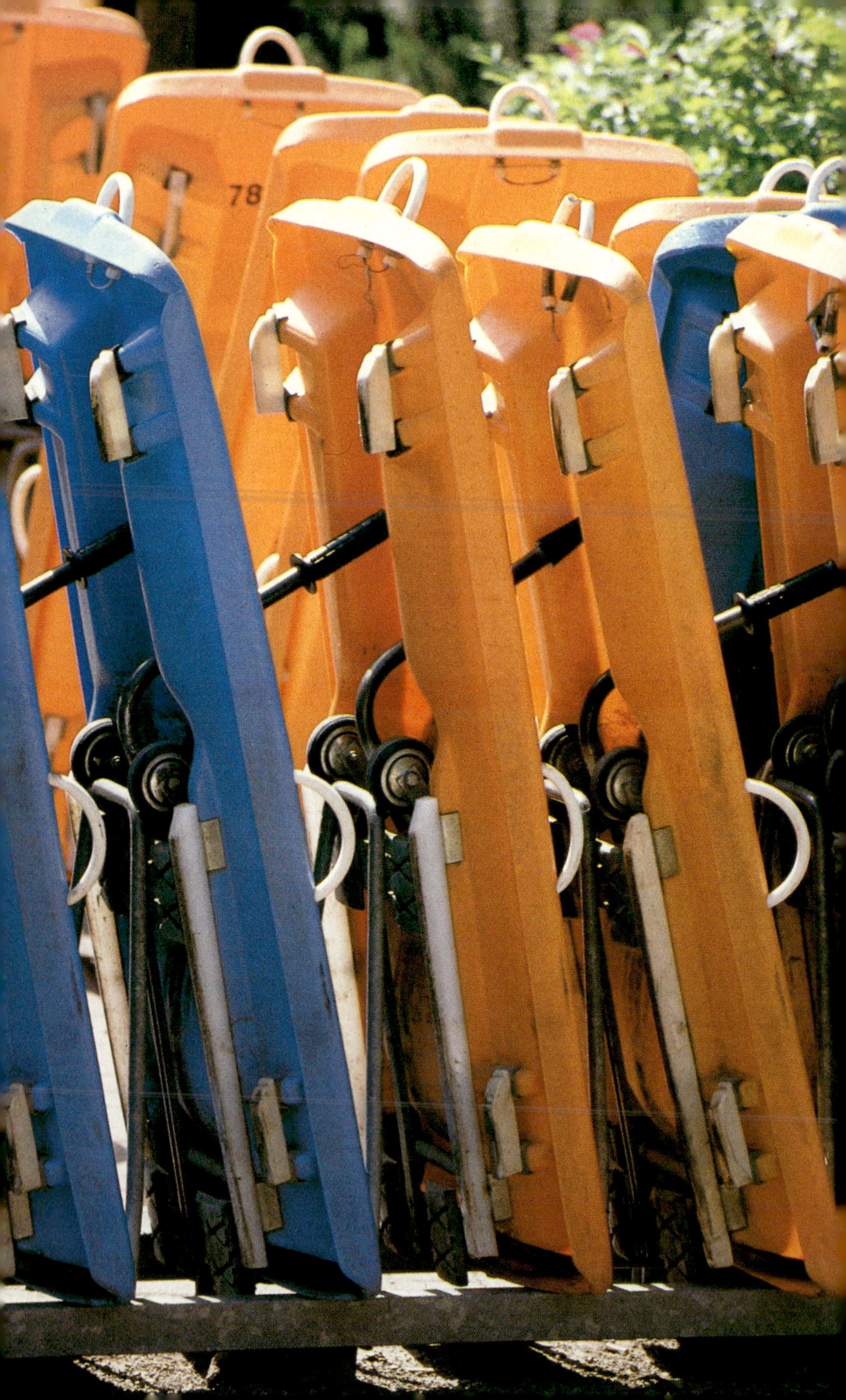
78

Information Centre 2: The Viewfinder of the SFX

The optical designers have put together a whole box of tricks to project the image so sharply and brilliantly in the viewfinder. The folding mirror is a mechanical masterpiece! Extremely light in weight for fast and rapid reaction, and absolutely rigid – the right pre-conditions for a precisely-defined image on the focusing screen. The centre of the mirror is partially transparent to let through an exactly defined and measured beam of light to be reflected from an auxiliary mirror situated at the back of the camera. This latter mirror redirects the beam, which represents a small section from the subject, to the bottom of the camera towards the autofocus sensor. The thin, dark lines that look like a spider's web, which you can see when the lens is removed, are not there just for decoration. They are coatings between the layers of the mirror to ensure that the light is uniformly distributed to the viewfinder. As a result of this and other technical advances the viewfinder of the SFX produces as bright an image as other Pentax models without the AF facility. I would advise you though to curb your

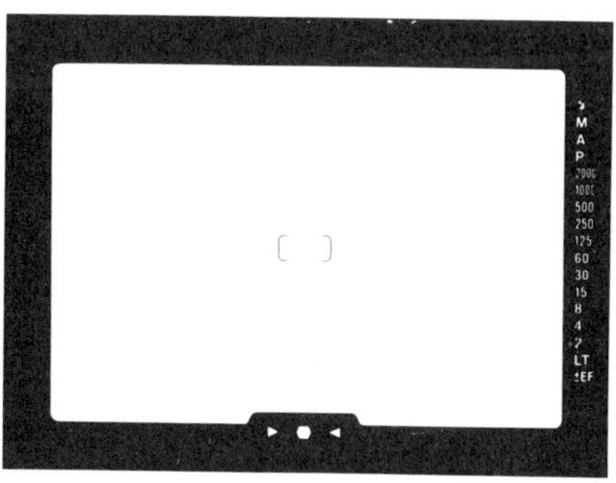

All the necessary information in the viewfinder. The viewfinder image is clear and unencumbered; no displays, no metering aids.

The long focal length makes this mundane subject worth a fresh look; the backlight adds the accent. *Photo: Richard Hünecke*

curiosity and don't poke the mirror: its repair could make a nasty hole in your pocket!

You should have noticed something when looking through the viewfinder for the first time: the usual focusing aids such as split image indicator and microprism ring are absent. Macro enthusiasts and users of extremely long focal length lenses will not shed a tear at their absence, such "aids" are more of a hindrance than a help in these special fields. As the SFX performs all focusing operations automatically you do not need any aids at all. The fine frame outlining the autofocusing zone is no hindrance to the macro or long-telephoto photographer. If the situation arises when you want to focus your AF or A lens by eye, then you will find the focusing screen in the SFX an excellent partner. This has been produced by a new process and is very easy to use, and it is a sheer joy to assess the focus, even with short focal lengths.

It is also possible to adapt your viewfinder to particular photographic tasks by exchanging the focusing screen for another one. This is done in the usual manner through the bayonet opening. Two types are available:

- ***FG-40***: focusing screen with AF metering field and line grid for exact alignment in architectural and reprographic photography.
- ***FD-41***: clear focusing screen with an index at the centre, specially useful for microscopy and extreme macro photography where focusing on the aerial image has to be done manually.

These focusing screens are made by high precision techniques from high quality material. They are very delicate and should not be touched. Put aside your well-laundered handkerchief; use a very soft brush, which has been squeezed for some minutes in an anti-static cloth, to brush away the odd speck of dust.

Those of you who wear glasses will be very glad of the little slider on the eyepiece. This is the dioptre correction for correcting eyesight deficiencies between +1.5 to -1.5 dioptres. Point the camera at a uniformly bright area devoid of detail,

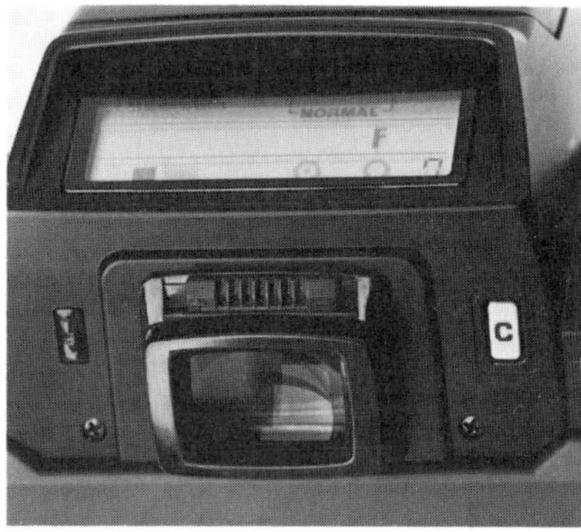

The little slide switch at the upper edge of the viewfinder eyepiece allows eyesight corrections from +1.5 to -1.5 dioptres. On the left of the eyepiece is the LED display for the metering flash; to the right is the C button.

such as a white ceiling, and move the slider to the right or left until you see the frame of the AF metering area in sharp focus. If you cannot achieve sharp focus you need a bigger dioptre correction for which you can get separate correction lenses to attach to the eyepiece. However, in this case you will have to forgo the soft rubber eyepiece shield because the guide grooves will be occupied by the correction lens. The soft rubber shield is one of the nicest things that I have set my face against for a long time. It fits pleasantly against the eye, affording good protection against stray light, regardless of whether you use your right or your left eye, in horizontal or in upright format. In addition, the slider for eyepiece adjustment is protected from accidental changes in its setting.

The viewfinder of the SFX shows 92% of the picture area. This corresponds approximately to the format of a framed slide if the AF 50mm, f/1.4 lens is set to infinity and the eyepiece is set to -1 dioptres, giving a reproduction scale of 0.81x..

The information given in the viewfinder is limited to the necessary data: the shutter speed from $^1/_2$ to $^1/_{2000}$ second, and "A", "P" or "M" for the selected shooting mode. These data are displayed for about 12 seconds after the finger has let go of the release button. Below the viewfinder are three electronic focusing control LEDs. Next to the eyepiece, at the left, is the flash-ready lamp for the integrated flash.

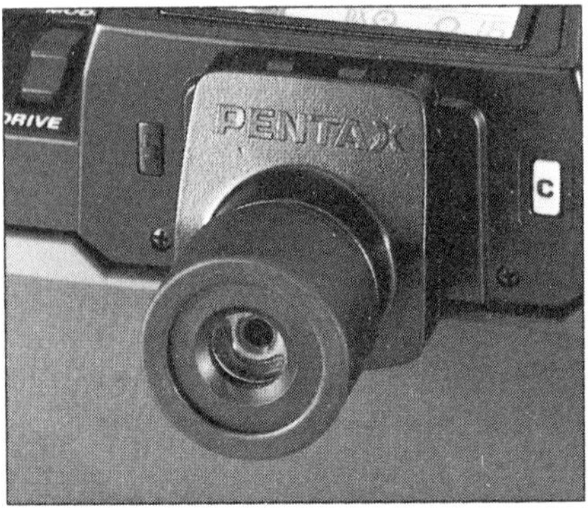

Viewfinder magnifier giving 1.62-times magnification of the central section of the viewfinder image.

The ***Focusing Lens F*** accessory may be pushed from the side into the eyepiece grooves. This enlarges the centre of the viewfinder image by 1.62 times. Its eyepiece may be adjusted from +4 to –1 dioptres. This is particularly useful for focusing on details adjacent to the AF frame when long focal-length lenses are used in the extreme macro range, provided the subject is immobile and the camera position is fixed. To assess the overall image, the magnifying lens is simply swung aside to reveal the whole image through the viewfinder.

Another interesting accessory from the earlier Pentax system is the Anglefinder A. This can be pushed over the eyepiece and is very convenient for macro work. It is very satisfying to be able to continue to use an accessory from your earlier outfit. Its tube may be turned about the viewfinder axis and its eyepiece is adjustable from +4 to -4 dioptres. The viewfinder image is shown the right way up and the right way round. The viewing ratio is 1:1, but this may be increased to a magnification of 2:1 for the centre of the screen. If you have ever cricked your neck when taking close-ups with your camera screwed to a tabletop tripod you will appreciate this gadget. It is not only for reproduction, there are other situations when it is useful, such as when you are waiting with your cat for a mouse to appear from its hole, or sitting in the damp grass observing the mysterious goings-on of nature.

Then there are the candid shots which you can bring off by hiding your camera under your arm and taking a surreptitious shot sideways with your AF 70-210mm zoom.

The only item still needed is the eyepiece cover. This is essential when using the camera on a tripod. Normally your head shields the eyepiece from stray light, which can enter this way into the pentaprism and cause incorrect meter readings, but if you are using a remote release, or not looking through the eyepiece, it must be shielded when the camera is metering the light. The hot shoe cover on the SFX serves as the eyepiece cover. Remove it from the hot shoe and slide it onto the eyepiece in place of the soft rubber frame. Should you find yourself frantically looking for this little item, check the parking slit on the AF 400 FTZ flashgun!

SAFOX Ensures Sharpness

So what is SAFOX? It stands for "Sensory Ability Fortifying Optical Compensation System". This is what it says in the technical specification for the SFX. A closer look at the detailed description of the autofocus system should make things a little clearer. SAFOX is an optical-electronic system which is supposed to increase the sharpness-perception of the image sensor. The first few test shots will convince you of this. One other thing: it has probably occurred to you that SAFOX was further abbreviated down to SFX to provide the model description for the camera.

SAFOX ensures that the microprocessor controlling the functions of the autofocus motor enables it to focus the lens on the subject plane quicker and more precisely, than can be achieved by the combination of eye, brain and hand. The highest reproduction qualities of the lens, the quietest subject and the most rigidly supported camera are all of no avail if the distance setting is inaccurate – the final picture will be unsharp.

Concerning the Difficulty in Defining Sharpness

We all know from experience what a picture looks like when it is not in sharp focus. We need no defined classification of unsharpness to tell us that it is only fit for the wastepaper basket. Unsharpness can be avoided in several ways. Against camera shake we use fast to very fast shutter speeds, or we support the camera on a tripod. For a fast-moving subject we use a fast shutter speed 1/500 second or faster. But the distance is constantly changing and very fast focusing is necessary to keep up, and for that we need help.

If the horse is dozing in the afternoon sun, its headgear may be the better subject. AF 70-210mm Zoom. Photo: Richard Hünecke

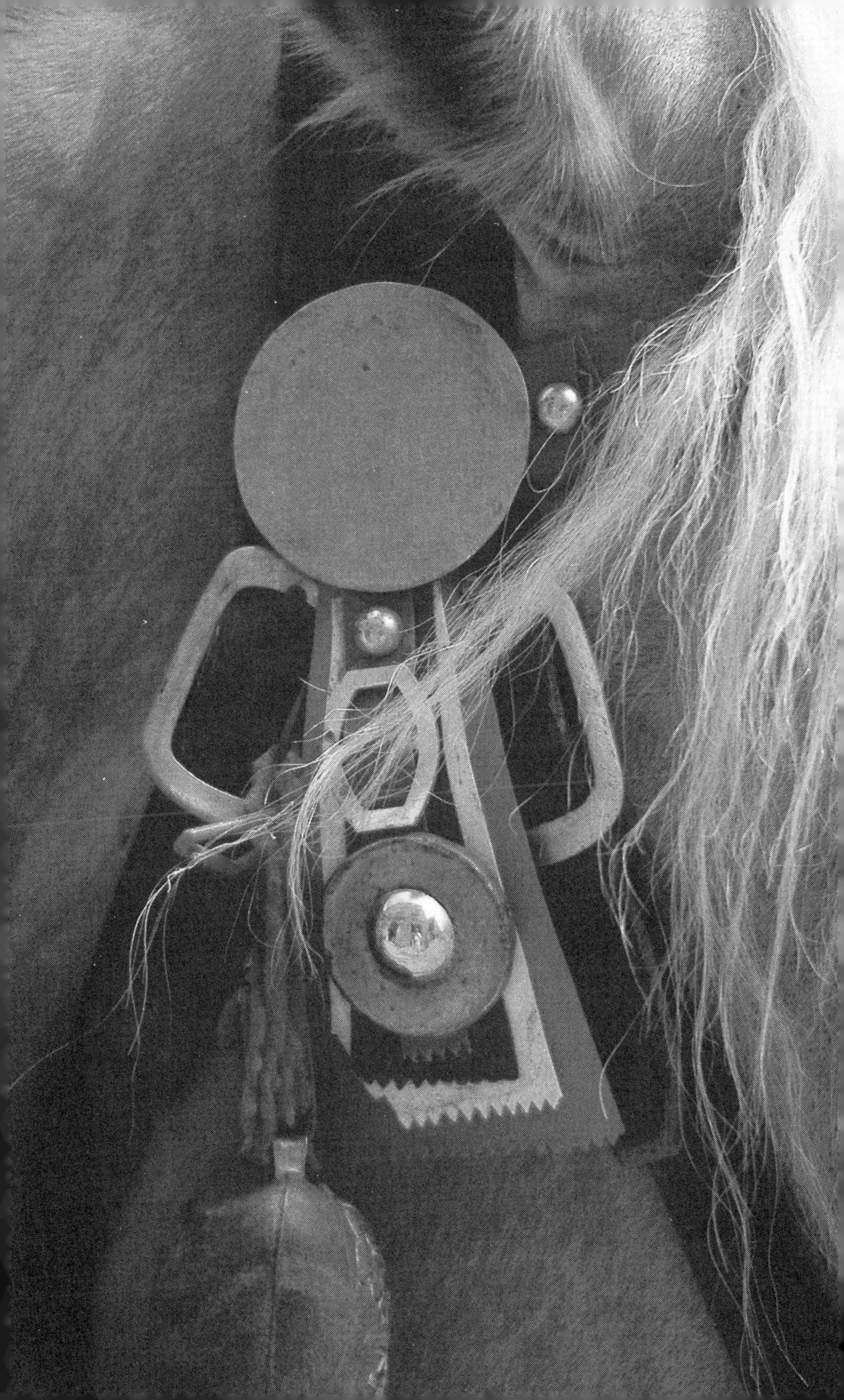

I shall discuss this in a minute. First I am going to deal with the question of what is sharpness and how can it be defined. Physicists and optical designers have still not arrived at a definition that suits the photographer's concept of pin-sharp focus. We shall therefore have to content ourselves with a few facts from our photographic experience.

Because of the wave nature of light it is impossible for a projected image to represent a point in a subject as a true point. The image of the point will show a microscopic transition from black to grey to white. Take for example the black and white squares of a chess board. In reality the black and white squares butt onto each other without an intermediate grey zone, but in their projected image there will be a narrow zone ranging from pale, to medium, to dark grey as one moves across the boundary from a white square to a black one. The width of the narrow transition zone will depend on the reproduction quality of the lens, but it is not the only factor. The further the point of focus from the film plane, the more "diffused" will be the representation on the film – the broader the "grey" zone between the black and the white squares of the chessboard. At some point this effect will become visible to the human eye in, for instance, a 30x45cm (12x18in) print from the normal reading distance of 30cm (12in).

You are already familiar with the two associated conditions for "picture sharpness": an image appears sharper and smoother on the small screen of a portable television you might take with you on a camping holiday than on the large screen of the set in your living room if they are both viewed from the same distance. But looking at the television in the living room from the other side of the room it will look sharp to you. More or less the same applies to your 50x75cm print. Viewed from a distance equivalent to at least twice the picture diagonal, it will look sharp, provided it was properly focused and not blurred due to camera shake and the processing lab has done it justice. The problem of sharpness is usually of minor importance in prints of the popular size of 10x15cm, unless the focusing was really poor, but the moment of truth arrives if you decide to get a few of your better holiday negatives enlarged to 45x67.5cm.

Focusing Control – Then and Now

Photography is an ageless hobby. Everything you may have learnt a long time ago is still applicable today. At one time a pocket camera, focused for a medium distance and using an aperture of f/8 would produce reasonable results because the large depth of field would accommodate any errors in focusing. However, when the lenses of pocket cameras became much faster the wider aperture values could no longer be used with estimated distance setting because of the resulting narrow depth of field. A rangefinder, combined with the viewfinder and coupled to the focusing, was soon incorporated as a standard feature on many pocket cameras from medium-priced models upwards. The rangefinder in the Leica M3/M6 has such high precision and reliability, even under poor lighting conditions, that it cannot be improved upon, even by electronic means. The triangulation principle of mechanical distance metering also forms the working principle of the modern optical-

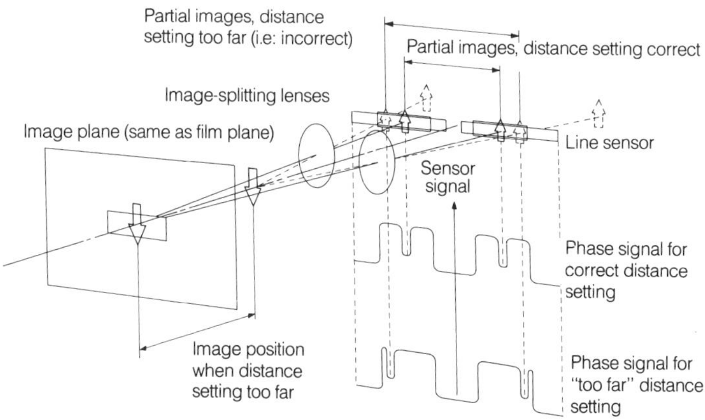

Diagram illustrating the principle of the phase comparison system used for automatic distance metering in the SFX.

electronic/mechanical pocket cameras with automatic focusing.

The modern SLR camera offers focusing aids in addition to the finely-structured focusing screen. These are the split image indicator and microprism ring, both of which are usually provided at the centre of the focusing screen. It was recognised that focusing on the focusing screen alone, despite viewfinder magnification or prismatic focus finders, was not the best possible method in the very early years of the SLR camera – about 50 years ago. The split image indicator, consisting of two wedge elements arranged in such a way that their plane surfaces cross in the plane of the focusing screen, is useful for focusing on edges and lines that cross the line separating the wedges at right angles to it. Turning the focusing ring causes the two halves of the split image to move against each other. The lens is properly focused on that portion of the image whose lines are shown unbroken in the split image indicator, i.e. its lines will be properly aligned between the two halves. Lines running at an oblique angle to the centre line of

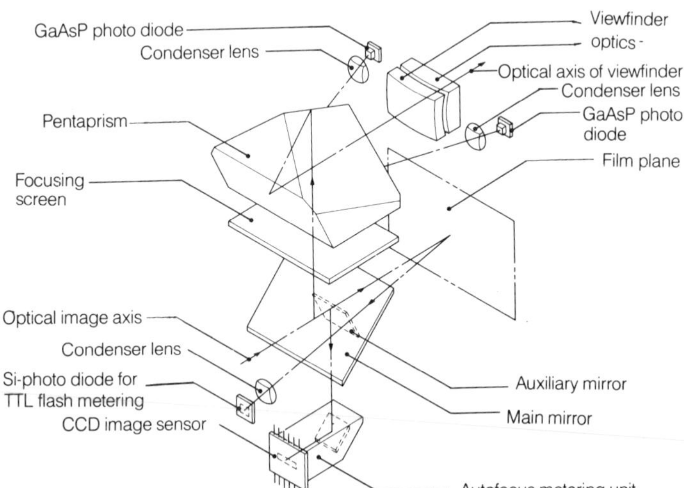

Path of the light rays through the automatic distance and light metering system

the indicator are not quite so easy and reliable to use. The more oblique the angle of the lines, or the more confusing the structure of the image, the more difficult it is to use the split image indicator. For such subjects the microprism ring performs more satisfactorily. The pyramid-shaped microprisms show an out-of focus subject flickering and scattered, whereas a properly-focused subject will be seen clear and sharp. Both of these focusing aids give their best performance with fast lenses. For lenses with largest apertures of f/5.6 and smaller these aids are more of a hindrance than a help. One half of the split image indicator turns partially dark and the structure of the microprism ring becomes very noticeable. Focusing precision also depends on the photographer's ability to adapt to the -1 dioptre correction applied to the eyepiece, which has been adopted for most camera systems. If one's individual eyesight varies too greatly from this value, then it will be difficult to focus.

The SFX Focuses with Sensor and Chip

The focusing screen is now produced by laser technology. Split image indicator and microprism ring have been improved and perform better now with slower lenses. But these advances did not constitute the improvement that all those who had problems with the focusing control on the SLR were waiting for. We had to wait a little longer for the introduction of optical-electronics and high precision mechanics, which together produce an automatic focusing system that combines control of the lens setting. The basic principle appears simple at first sight. The partially-translucent mirror directs a precisely defined amount of light onto the auxiliary mirror at the camera back. The auxiliary mirror transfers this portion of the subject onto the light-sensitive surface of the CCD image sensors. These transmit the sharp/unsharp impression as electronic signals to the computer. The computer makes its calculations

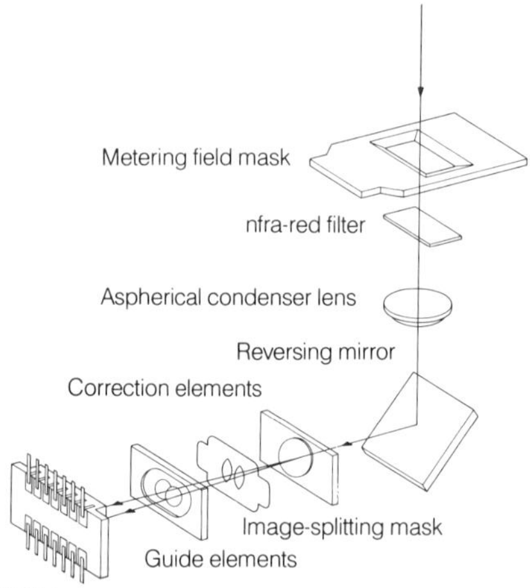

Diagram of internal construction of SAFOX focusing sensor

and sends the appropriate messages to the autofocus motor. This moves the lens helix by so-many revolutions which focuses the lens exactly on the subject plane corresponding to the autofocus metering square at the centre of the viewfinder screen. The Pentax SFX follows this well-accepted principle, with the addition of a few refinements.

The light diverted from the auxiliary mirror is exactly delineated by a field mask. It passes through an infra-red filter to remove any infra-red light, then through a condenser lens and a correction lens to remove some reproduction errors. The subject detail, outlined by the AF-metering frame, is then projected onto a plane equivalent to the film plane. Two image-splitting lenses, behind the image splitting mask, divide the projected image into two parts and transfer the result onto two CCD line sensors. The reproduction system, accommodated in a tiny space at the bottom of the camera, is capable of transmitting to the CCD image sensor an extremely clear image, free of any reproduction errors, that represents the focusing conditions presented to the lens.

If the focusing is correct, the two partial images produced by the image-splitting unit always lie at the same position, namely the zero position of the line sensors. If the subject is focused on a greater distance, then the distance between the two partial images is larger. It is smaller than the distance for the zero position if the lens is focused too close. From the size and direction of the phase shift the AF computer calculates the number and direction of the revolutions of the AF motor necessary to correct the focusing. The very cleverly designed compensation system in the AF circuit ensures that even the minutest phase differences are properly perceived and the necessary fine adjustment made.

To brake the lens focusing mechanism at exactly the right moment when it is in "full flight", for it to come to rest at precisely the specified spot, is quite an art. To succeed in this means the speed would have to be constantly checked, reduced near the target point, and, if necessary, checked shortly before. The autofocus computer performs this task in the following way. It divides the revolutions that the motor has to turn into precisely defined partial amounts and stores this number. A sensor reads a 28-digit code disc on the second gear shaft and transmits the revolution impulses to the AF computer which then compares it with the stored value. At a certain number of remaining impulses the AF computer follows the count-down so that the motor stops exactly after the final impulse as it is read off the code disc – the AF lens is precisely focused!

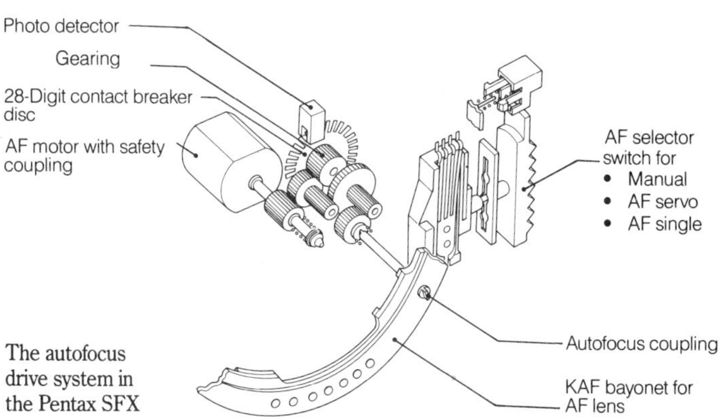

The autofocus drive system in the Pentax SFX

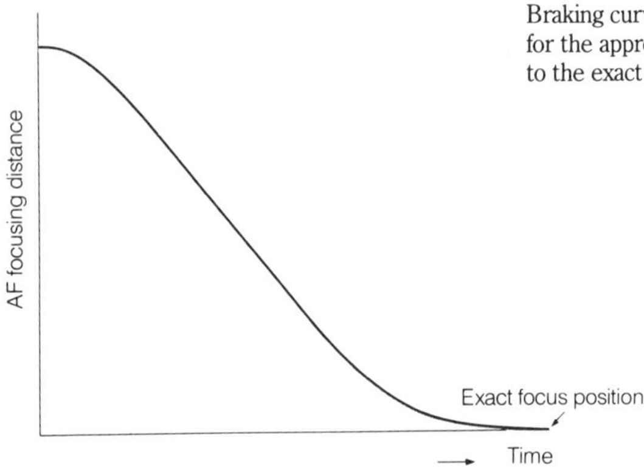

Braking curve of the AF motor for the approach of the AF lens to the exact focus position

The AF computer does not leave it at that. It then makes a control measurement to check whether the calculated lens movement was properly performed. If this is found to be satisfactory, then the AF system has finished its task. If it detects a difference to its calculated setting, then it immediately effects a correction. Should the helical gear in the lens have arrived at one of its limit stops during or before this point, then the safety coupling on the motor shaft engages and stops the movement, thus preventing any damage to the lens. As the 28-digit code disc stops at the same time it is unable to send any counting impulses to the photo-detector and the AF motor switches off.

The Performance Range of the AF Computer

The phase shift of the two partial images in the sensor lines is the information that the AF computer uses to formulate the number of revolutions for the AF motor. But life is not as simple as that: the calculation has to be suitable for the AF lens that is currently attached to the bayonet. The AF computer needs some personal data from the lens. Part of this information could come from the contacts in the KA bayonet, i.e. the maximum aperture of the lens. But the lens data have to be presented in a different form for exposure metering and automatic exposure control than for automatic focusing. What the AF computer has to know in order to perform its task is programmed into the ROM chip of every AF lens: these are lens speed, focal length and, in the case of AF zooms, also the variable focal lengths as well. The computer avails itself of this information via the seventh contact in the bayonet, which was added to the KA mount as the autofocus development. The information stored in the ROM chip in the lens, and made available through the other contacts on the AF lens, is passed to the microprocessor in the SFX. If the attached lens is an A-lens, then the seventh contact in the camera cannot detect its counterpart on the lens and activates only the well-known A-functions of the exposure control.

Now the relationship between the autofocus sensor and the exposure meter in the SFX also becomes clear. Both need a certain amount of light to perform their task and both work within certain limit points of too little or too much light. The upper limit of the autofocus sensor is EV18 at ISO 100/21°, which corresponds to 1/2000 second at f/11, or 1/500 second at f/22, or 1/125 second at f/32. This does not mean that the AF sensor immediately packs up as soon as this value is reached, but that that much light blinds the AF sensor and interferes with its performance.

Exposure value 2, i.e. 1/2 second at f/1.4 or 2 seconds at f/2.8 at ISO 100/21° is the official lower limit for the AF sensor. Here too is a similar situation as that with the upper limit. It is still capable of performing but its functioning is no longer as reliable and precise. Your own experiences will be very similar under these conditions. How well the AF sensor performs under poor lighting conditions depends on the subject contrast. Dark railings against a white background supply sufficient contrast even under EV0.5 (1.5 seconds at f/1.4) and the AF sensor will not hesitate to give you a perfect focus. But if you are trying to focus on a pale-yellow silk ribbon against a white wall, then the AF sensor will send the focusing helix through the entire focusing range from close-up to infinity and back again, and then stop its activities because it comes to the conclusion that further attempts are pointless.

Lighting aid for the AF sensor

But all is not lost. For these situations the SFX has a metering beam next to the built-in flashgun in the pentaprism. If the subject brightness drops to EV5 (at ISO 100/21°) or below, then an intense infra-red LED with aspherical optical element automatically emits a striped light/dark pattern when the release is depressed. This provides the AF sensor with a target as a suitable focusing point, even on completely featureless surfaces and in complete darkness. How you would overcome the problem of actually selecting the framing of the subject in complete darkness is another matter. The power of the metering flash is sufficient for a subject at 4m distance. I have just tested it in a fairly dark room on a not too dark subject with reasonable structures and found it worked

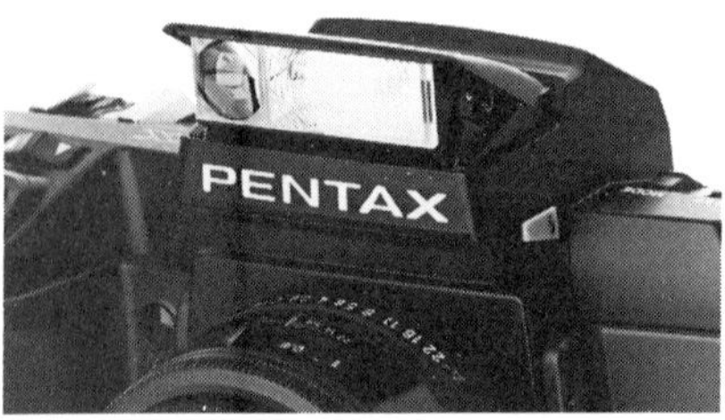

Light pressure on the release button is sufficient: the flash pops up and after only a few seconds the red light metering flash is ready for use

---

Top: No great depth of field is required for architectural details such as this so an aperture of f/5.6 is sufficient. Even if the lighting conditions are not favourable this provides enough leeway to keep the shutter speed fast enough for the long focal length used here. AF 70-210mm Zoom.
Photo: Richard Hünecke

Bottom: If you have an AF 1.7X adapter for use with SMC-A lenses on the SFX, why not try it with the AF 70-210mm Zoom? Stopping down by at least 2 f/stops, this combination will produce a 119-357mm, f/6.8-9.5 lens with quite acceptable reproduction quality. *Photo: Richard Hünecke*

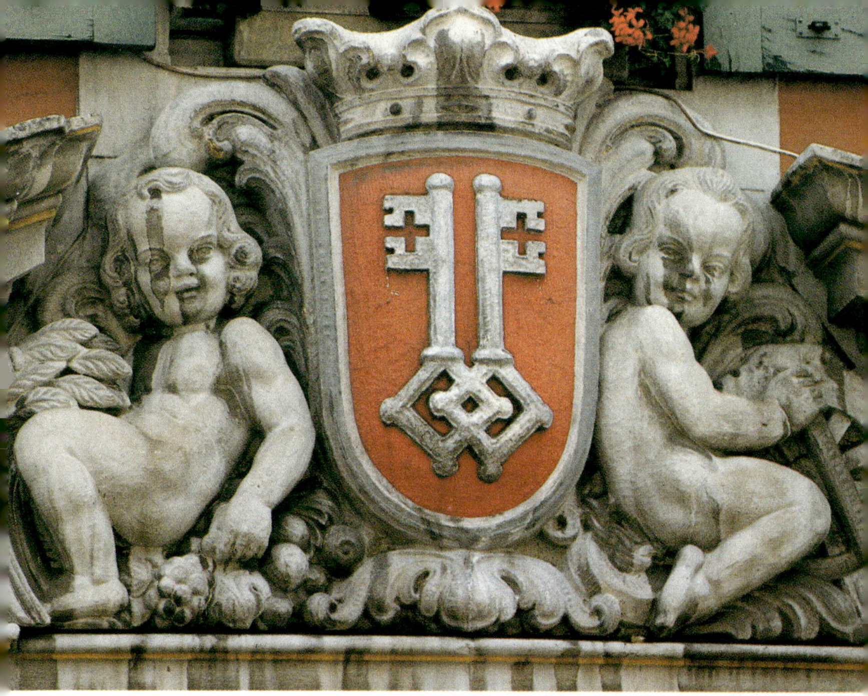

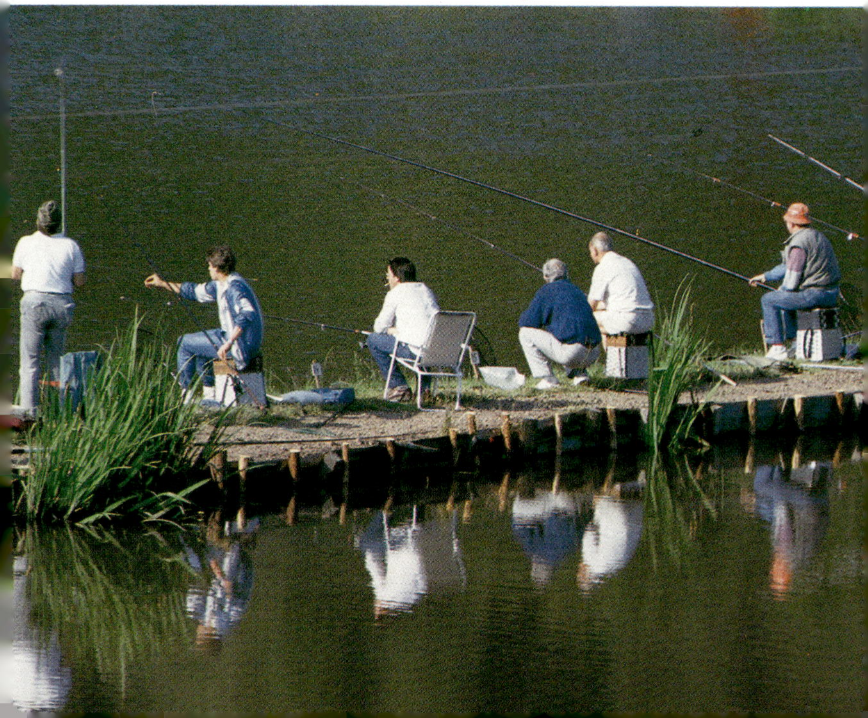

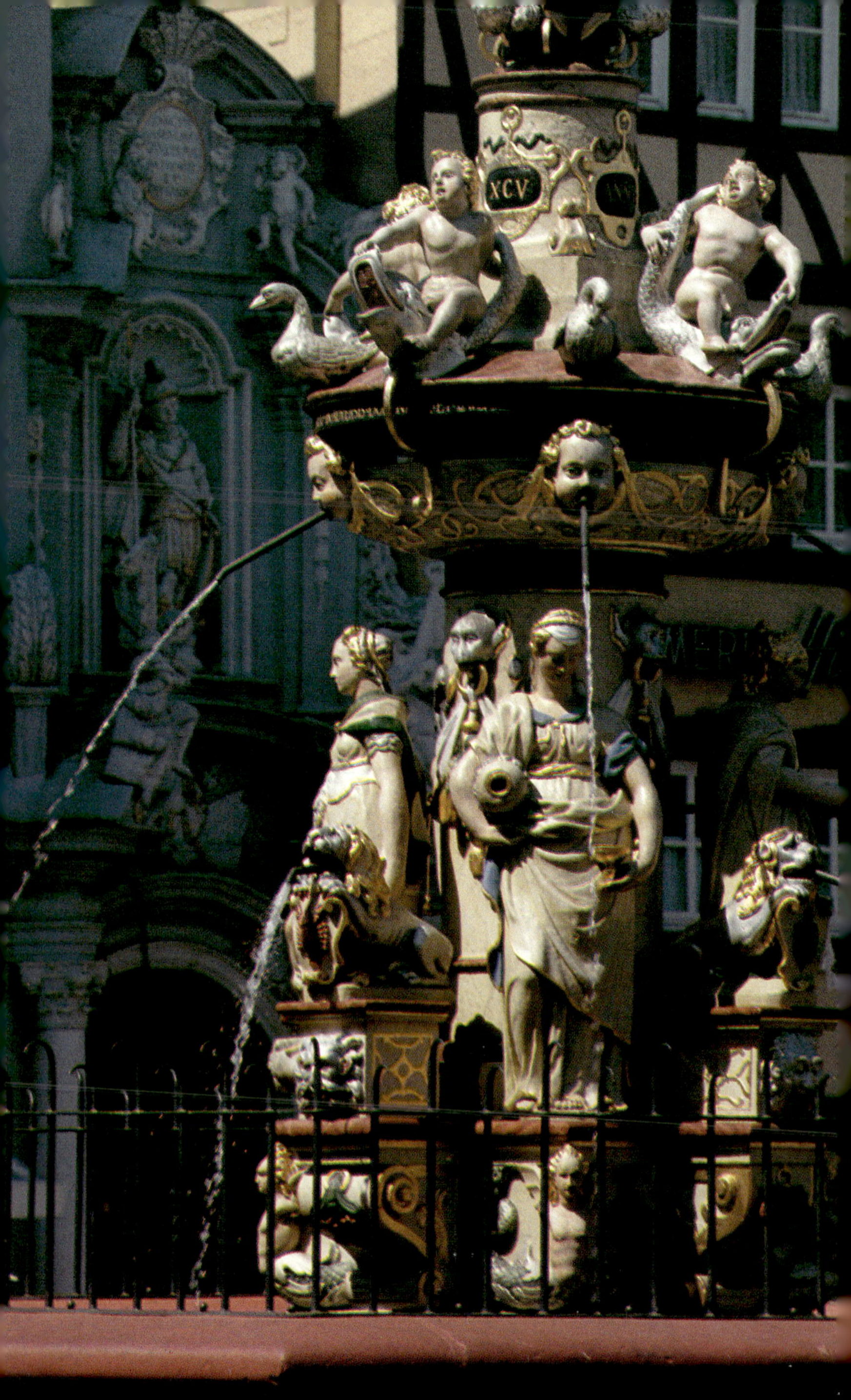
XCV

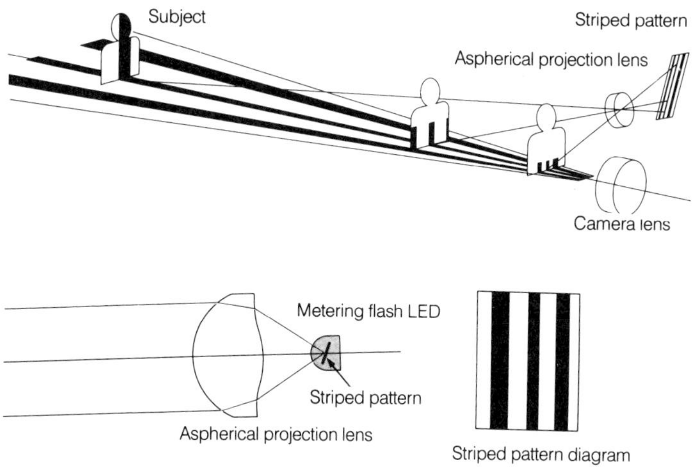

In poor lighting conditions the TAP system projects a striped pattern onto the subject and this is used for distance metering by the AF sensor.

quite satisfactorily to $5^{1}/_{2}$m. This TAP – Tilted Aspherical Projection – metering flash can be used together with the integrated flash, or with any other flashgun attached to the hot shoe of the SFX. The TAP can also be used on its own, without flash, if you do not want to disturb the mood of an available light scene and are shooting with very fast films. If the green focusing indicator in the viewfinder illuminates then you simply return the miniflash to its cap, keep the focusing position locked by depressing the "ML" button and then release. A more potent metering flash is available with the Pentax AF 400 FTZ flashgun. The metering flash in this unit also works according to the TAP principle and is officially rated to function to a subject distance of 7m. However, under the above-mentioned conditions it will manage even as far as 10m! You can use this flashgun also simply as a metering flash to assist the

---

This fountain is shown to good effect in the afternoon or early evening. The sun falling at an angle picks out the water to better effect than when it is directly overhead at midday. AF 70-210mm Zoom. Photo: Richard Hünecke

AF sensor; the shot itself may then be taken under the available light.

The autofocus system of the SFX is not satisfied with just one metering flash. The metering function is checked by a second and even third metering flash if it is not absolutely sure that it has achieved a satisfactory result. The focus of the lens is then adjusted if the subsequent reading establishes a difference. Under such difficult conditions the focusing process will take a little longer than usual, but I am sure you will be patient in such cases.

The excellent responsiveness of the autofocus sensor in the SFX, which is far in excess even of the limits ordinarily achieved with fast lenses, is also demonstrated in other areas. It will focus with the AF 50mm, f/1.4 and also the AF 35-70mm, f/3.5-4.0 Zoom on a 2mm wide black line against a matt-white background for a subject distance of 2m in diffuse, weak light (EV6 at ISO 100/21°). Under the same conditions it will focus with either lens on a 0.4mm fine line at a subject distance of 0.70m, in this case perhaps with a slight correction. If the metering sensor is unable to obtain a clear metering result and is therefore unable to focus the lens, then it will stop its activities and indicate this by the two inward pointing arrows in the viewfinder.

Electronic Focusing, with Variations

The autofocus system of the Pentax SFX offers several focusing modes, the three major ones of which are selected by the sliding focus-mode switch on the front of the camera body just to the right of the lens. The three positions of this switch are labelled; Manual, Servo, and Single, respectively. To select the manual mode it is necessary to keep pressed a small safety button immediately above this switch.

Some non-auto lenses such as the existing Pentax-A and M series can be used by focusing manually with the assistance of the focus indication system in the camera. The green in-focus signal lights up when the object aimed at is in focus and, if switched on, an audible signal sounds.

Non-autofocus lenses with a maximum aperture of f/2.8 and greater can be used in autofocus mode in conjunction with the autofocus adapter 1.7X. This is positioned between the camera body and the lens and is a 4-group, 6-element teleconverter with the necessary focusing movement incorporated. It increases the focal length of the prime lens by a factor of X1.7 and effective f/numbers are increased similarly. The AF adapter sets the correct distance for the attached lens but always within the limitations of its groups of lenses in the 5mm long mount.

SINGLE for general applications

Push the main switch to "I" and set the focus-mode switch to SINGLE. Point the SFX at the subject, so that the AF metering frame at the centre of the viewfinder screen covers the subject detail which has to be in sharp focus, and gently press the release button halfway down. The AF motor will set the correct focus for the subject and you should check the shutter speed at the right side of the viewfinder to ensure it is

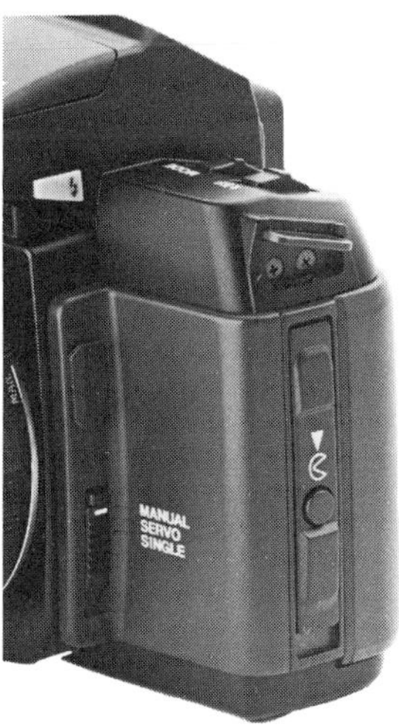

The autofocus switch of the SFX has three positions.

suitable. The green hexagon at the bottom of the viewfinder screen will give you the all-clear for the shot and you can then press the release all the way down to complete the process. If you press the release all the way down right at the start the camera will complete the same procedure: first it will focus the lens, then it will release the shutter to take the shot.

If, for example, you are too close to the subject so that the close-up limit for that particular lens is exceeded, or the subject is totally featureless so that the autofocus system has no clear indication of whether it has focused, then the AF computer will activate the lens, to search for a focus, making it travel from close-up to infinity and back again, after which it will stop trying. If it was unable to focus because the subject was too close, then the right-hand red arrow at the base of the viewfinder will light up. If the lens can't focus because of a featureless subject, both arrows will light up and the release will be locked. Even if you try to jam down the release the autofocus system is always in control and the release will be locked because SINGLE means focus priority, i.e. the shutter may be released only if perfect focus is obtained.

The autofocus sensor reacts only to the small subject section outlined by the focusing frame at the centre of the viewfinder. If you want to show the triumphant pose of the goalkeeper in sharpest focus, but don't want to place him at the centre of the frame, then you proceed as before but keep the release button slightly pressed, realign the camera to the required framing and then release the shutter. This is the way you obtain focus lock with the SFX. However, if the footballer jumps a couple of steps forward at the moment you release, then your picture will be spoilt. In this case you would have to take your finger off the release button, take a new reading, and then release again. The focus lock is useful for a variety of subjects. If you are observing a group of people in deep conversation with their heads together, you focus on the important detail first, and then realign the frame, otherwise the wall in the background would be sharp, and the important figures lower in the frame would be blurred.

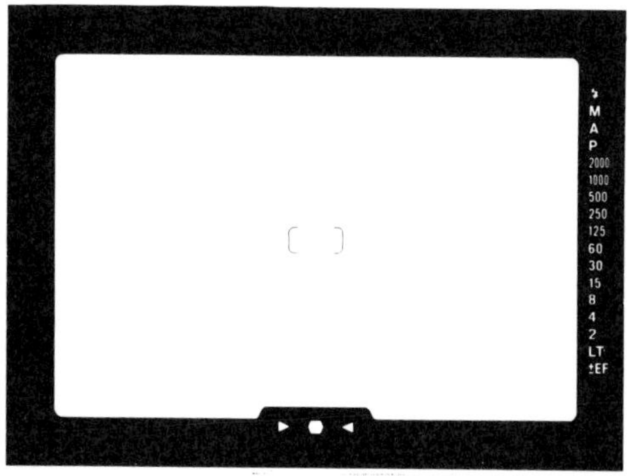

The focusing LEDs and the information displayed in the viewfinder of the SFX.

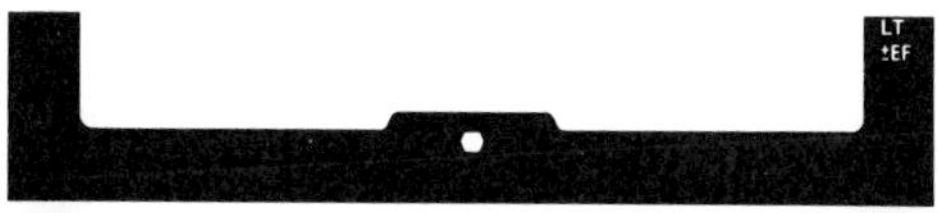

Correct focus

Distance setting too close

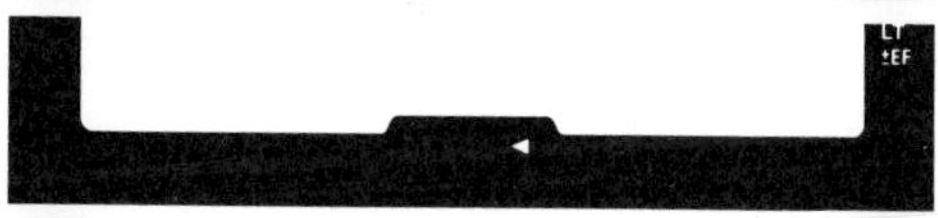

Distance setting too far

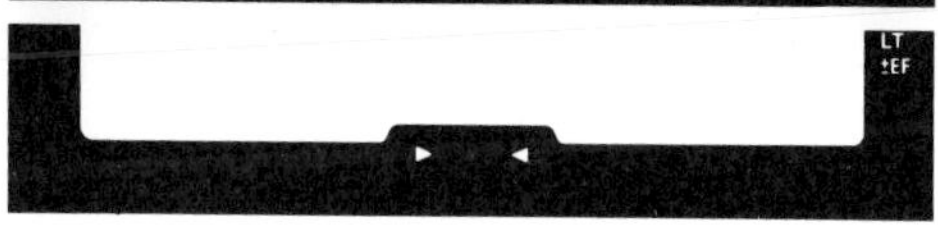

Correct focus impossible

If, on the other hand, you have used the DRIVE and select switches to set the camera to sequence shooting, then the autofocus computer will check the focus before each shot in the series. If the focus is correct, or only a slight adjustment is necessary, you will be shooting at approximately 2 frames per second. If the athlete has moved some distance during the film transport then the AF computer will adjust the setting accordingly. If the re-focusing takes longer than the 0.4 seconds interval between the shots, then the SFX cannot maintain the 2 frames per second sequence. It is vital to remember when shooting in SERIES mode that the important detail, the chest of the leader of the crowd of children in the playground, or whatever you are hunting at the time, is always kept in the centre of the viewfinder. If you can't keep up with the movement and the AF metering field covers something else, then the AF computer will immediately adjust for that setting and you will have lost the flow of the sequence. It is a good idea to limit yourself to short sequences and take your finger off the release after three or so shots. After all, you can always press your finger down again as soon as the scene appears to be interesting. The focus priority rule also applies in the SINGLE sequence mode. The computer will allow the shutter release to be triggered only if perfect focusing is obtained on the subject in the focusing frame. It therefore depends which is faster, the AF focusing process or the sprinter, as to whether you get a picture or not. Because of its very short focusing times the SFX will provide you with excellent chances to catch that perfect shot. Of course some luck is always useful but the facilities of the SFX will soon make it a favourite amongst sports, action and animal photographers!

SERVO even faster – or is it?

The small movement of the focus-mode switch from SINGLE to SERVO does not change any of the metering, control, and setting functions of the autofocus motor, it only cancels the requirement of no focus – no picture! In SERVO mode the AF system in the SFX reacts, with a partially-pressed release button, to any change in the subject distance with a correction to the focus setting. As soon as the AF sensor has fixed the focusing plane the green indicator will light up in the viewfinder. This is quite easy to see, even if you are concentrating on the subject. You should press the shutter fully as soon as the green indicator tells you that the cyclist racing by is in sharp focus. To follow the final effort of the cyclist towards the finishing line is a tall order and will defeat the SFX just like other autofocus cameras now on the market – any autofocus system has its limitations. The reactions of the

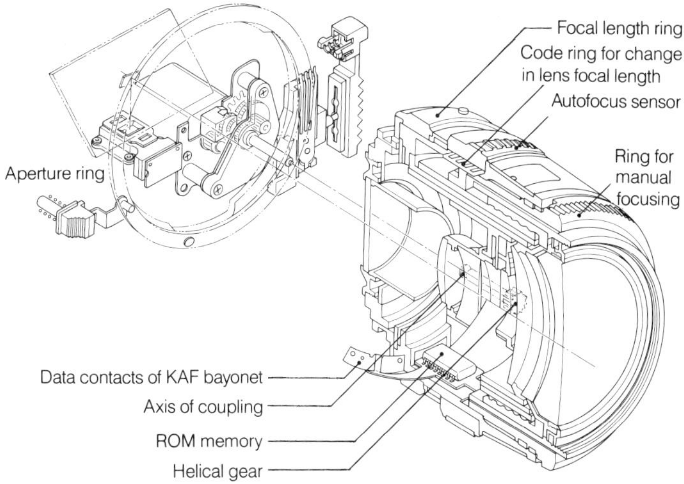

Cross-section through the AF mechanism from the AF motor in the SFX to the helical gear in the AF lens.

autofocus system to fast-moving subjects also depends greatly on the subject distance and focal length of the lens. It is therefore almost impossible to give clear, general information as to limits and results. You will have to try to assess the situation and the working limit of your SFX under various conditions.

If you don't always want to glance at the bottom of the viewfinder to check that proper focusing has been achieved you can set the main switch of the SFX to its top position. The AF computer will now confirm correct focusing by a intermittent high-pitched tone. In the SERVO setting of the AF mode there is no focus lock. This means that if you try to follow a footballer as he comes towards you and makes a fast turn to shake off his opponent, causing you to lose him from the AF metering field, then the SFX focusing system will react just as quickly and you will find that you have caught a wonderful shot of the spectators in the background, more or less sharply recorded, because in this mode it is possible to release the shutter, even if the AF function has not completed focusing.

For this reason the SERVO setting does not guarantee a sequence of sharp pictures in a series of action shots. I prefer to use it as a formula for precisely-selected individual shots or short sequences of up to four frames. This is best done by keeping the finger on the release in the half-way position while following the action, or the athlete as he sprints toward the springboard, and releasing at exactly the moment when the green indicator or the bleep tells you that the subject is in sharp focus. If you know the line the movement will take, then you can judge the right moment with little difficulty. Pressing the release button in SERVO mode you can catch both the point of take off and landing of the athlete competing in the long jump, provided of course, that your reactions are fast. Such a sequence is best taken in continuous shooting mode. One of the best features of the SFX is that you can select all these functions independently of the other operating modes.

CAMAF

This description is not limited to the Pentax SFX autofocus system. It is yet another of the short codes for "Computer Aided Manual Focusing" and it means the operation of the SFX when the focus-mode switch is set to MANUAL. To avoid any frustrating accidents this switch can be set to manual only when a locking button is pressed. The small step from SERVO to MANUAL separates the AF motor mechanically from the helical gear in the AF lens and electrically from the AF computer and electrical circuit. The AF sensor and the metering and computing functions in the AF computer with the three focusing LEDs in the viewfinder remain operative, and this makes manual focusing by the milled focusing ring on the lens quite straightforward. Because of the special construction of the AF lenses, focusing is easy and allows precise, fine adjustment by finger-tip control, even better than with any previous Pentax lens.

The focusing screen of the SFX differs from previous ones in that it is made to an optically high quality by modern methods. It is a joy to use for manual focusing – the image can be said to "jump" into sharp focus on the screen as soon as you set the correct distance. To focus on a subject that lies outside the AF metering field you can rely completely on the focusing screen; it is particularly well suited to focusing visually, both in the close-up and the distant ranges. Also, as its centre is free of any focusing aids such as a microprism ring or split field indicator, it is particularly suitable for macro shots and slow telephoto lenses.

The second variation for checking the focus in manual focusing mode is to bring the subject within the AF metering rectangle, press the release, and the LED arrows underneath the viewfinder will indicate whether your setting is too distant or too close. If the exact focusing point for the subject in the AF field is obtained, then the green in-focus indicator will light up and you know you can release the shutter. To save your having to constantly check the indicators in the viewfinder you can set the main switch to the top position and the audible indicator will sound when correct focus is obtained. Whether the audible indicator is of any assistance in automatic focusing, and in particular in the SERVO mode, is best left to your own decision.

Any of the AF lenses can be focused manually, aided by the LED indication, just as any Pentax lens with a K bayonet which also has to be focused in this manner. The only limitation for the CAMAF facility is that the speed of the lens has to be f/5.6 or greater.

Difficult Situations for the AF Computer

Any situation which causes problems to the human eye, split field indicator or microprism ring, is also difficult for the AF sensor. This could be the case with the cyclist who comes speeding down the final straight at an oblique angle towards you; if his movements are faster than even the rapidly-reacting AF function, then the automatic focusing will not be able to catch up with him and you will lose the race in the truest sense of the word. Even if you immediately push the release down in SINGLE mode the cyclist will have moved a few metres in the time it takes for the shutter to actually release, although this time is no longer than the blinking of an eye. If the SFX is set to consecutive advance the motor drive will activate a second and a third shot as long as the shutter release is kept depressed. The tiny focusing adjustment periods seem negligible during shooting, but you will be able to check later on when projecting your slides who was faster in this race, you or the cyclist. If you selected the audible indicator the number of sharp shots will entirely depend on the speed of your reaction to the audible signal. Here too you will have to wait to assess your success rate until the lab returns your pictures. A sequence taken in SERVO with continuous shooting will also depend to a large extent on whether the automatically-triggered release coincided with exact focusing. The shutter will release independently at a rate of two frames per second and the sequence could include a number of successful shots.

If the race between moving subject and autofocus computer is of the utmost importance then there is another trick that many sports photographers employ. Switch the SFX to continuous shooting mode and select manual focusing. Select a suitable focusing plane by focusing on an object at the distance that corresponds to the position where you expect the subject. At the moment when the cyclist is still about 3 or 4 metres away, press the release fully down for a sequence of, at the most, four shots. More is unnecessary because the cyclist will have moved about 30 metres in the three seconds up to the fifth shot. This is a good method, but even then you will have to accept a certain failure rate.

Subject structure

Presenting an absolutely uniformly structured subject to the SAFOX-boosted AF sensor will cause it the same problems as experienced by the manual focusing combination of eye/split-field indicator: both are unable, without any additional aids, to focus correctly. In the SINGLE mode the AF sensor will issue the command to block the release in keeping to the rule, no focus – no picture. In such a situation, for example a garden fence, a viewfinder screen with microprism indicator would be useful for manual focusing; the focus-mode first having been set to Manual. Or let's take the situation where you wish to photograph through a fence, taking a candid shot of the children playing in your neighbour's garden. In this case you have to be extra careful that the wooden fence lies outside the AF metering field, otherwise you would have a perfectly-focused fence in your picture, outlined against out-of-focus children.

If you offer the AF metering field two subject details at different distances to the camera, then it will not know which is the detail to focus on and will wander helplessly between the two focus settings. In this case you have to re-align the camera for one of these points to allow the AF sensor to select a setting.

Another structurally difficult subject is one whose lines are parallel with the longer sides of the AF metering rectangle. The problem here is the same as for focusing with a split-field indicator. There are two ways to remedy the situation: either you turn the camera to upright format and store the focus setting by keeping the release pressed until you have re-aligned the frame, or you change to manual focusing, checking visually on the focusing screen.

Then there is the featureless subject: the perfect skin of a young child under diffused, soft lighting may be attractive but the AF sensor will be thrown into confusion. It will traverse the focusing range from close-up to infinity and then signal its inability to find a suitable focusing point by stopping any further attempts. This is the situation for all featureless, uniformly-toned, subjects. The only way to overcome this difficulty is to switch to manual focusing. However, if the lighting conditions fall below EV5, then you can use the red metering flash from the integral mini-flash. If you also possess the Pentax AF 400 FTZ flashgun this will supply a suitable metering flash for all lighting conditions.

The positive metering characteristics of the AF sensor will usually disregard a reasonably clean window pane and focus perfectly on the subject behind it. However, focusing at an oblique angle through some double glazing will not be possible, because the double reflection of the four glass-air surfaces will confuse the metering system.

Star-burst and similar filters may upset the AF sensor, and the same applies to linear polarizing filters. If you want to use such filters you will have to focus manually. A circular polarizing filter is suitable for AF focusing.

Depth of Field Trap for Fast Shots

This function is only available with K- or KA-lenses. The lens has to be focused manually, with the LED indicator signalling whether your focusing is correct for the subject detail at the centre of the screen. If the focus-mode switch is left at SINGLE then the requirement of no focus – no picture will apply. This condition is exactly the facility that you can use to your own advantage. Focus the K- or KA lens on some pebbles at the side of the road, lift the camera to the shooting position and press the release fully: nothing happens until the first cyclist comes pedalling round the corner. You point the AF metering frame at his chest and the SFX will release as soon as the cyclist has moved to the pre-focused distance. The only thing to watch out for is the shutter speed which has to be fast enough to give you a shake-free shot. It is a pity that this most interesting and useful method cannot be used with AF lenses, but I assume that many of you will be using the Pentax SFX having moved on from an earlier Pentax system and your range of useful lenses will have been increased by keeping some well-tried earlier lenses.

The Pentax SFX Lenses

The newly-developed AF lenses for the SFX, SFX_N and SF7 cameras are altogether smoother than the previous Pentax SMC lenses. However there is still plenty of space for safe handling. The wide ring used for manual focusing has been reduced to a narrower one towards the front of the lens; this is because the automatic functions of the camera usually perform all the actual settings, manual focusing being reserved for just a few special situations. The ring had to be kept as narrow as possible to keep to a minimum the risk of interfering with the fast movements of the automatic focusing by the AF motor. A safety slip coupling prevents damage to the delicate gearings should a heavy finger accidentally touch the ring whilst the

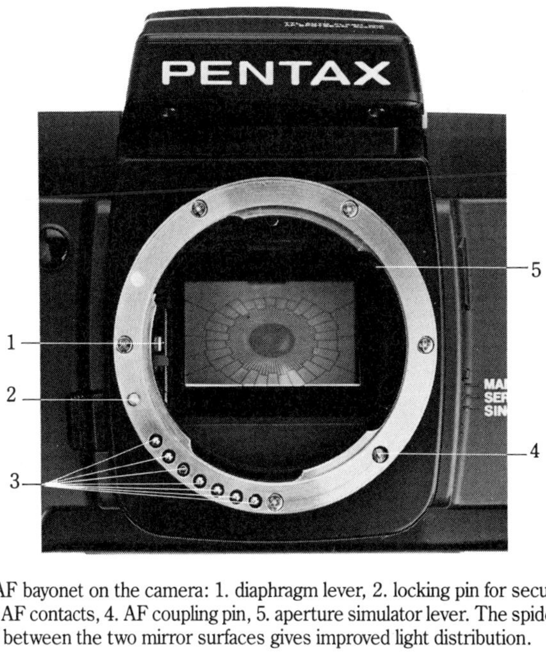

The KAF bayonet on the camera: 1. diaphragm lever, 2. locking pin for securing the lens, 3. AF contacts, 4. AF coupling pin, 5. aperture simulator lever. The spider's web pattern between the two mirror surfaces gives improved light distribution.

automatic focusing function is in motion. Then there is the aperture ring, which – unlike other SLR manufacturers – Pentax have retained for manual aperture selection. This has proved to be no disadvantage whatsoever.

It is precisely the presence of this aperture ring why all previous Pentax lenses with K and KA bayonets will fit the KAF bayonet of the SF7, SFX and SFX_N cameras. Pentax have retained the basic form of the KA bayonet; the aperture lever, which transfers the manually selected aperture value from the lens to the camera is therefore also present as is the second lever for diaphragm function. The only difference from the KA bayonet is the extra contact, i.e. instead of the six contacts there are now seven. Then there is the slotted coupling for the follower pin of the motor drive. This adaptation makes the K

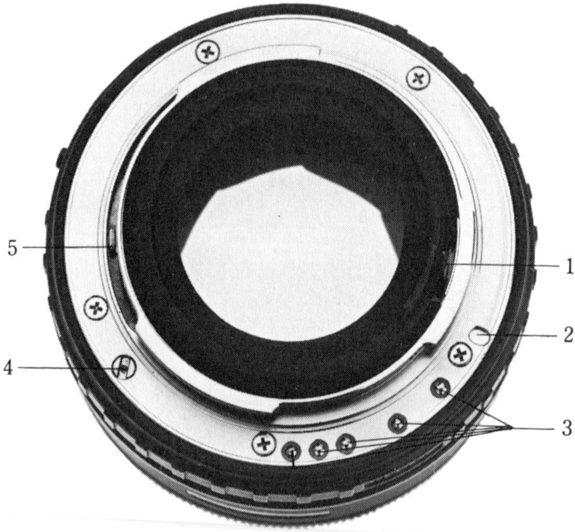

KAF bayonet on the lens: 1. diaphragm lever, 2. notch to accommodate lens locking pin, 3. AF contacts, 4. AF coupling, 5. aperture simulator; transfers the aperture value selected on the lens to the camera's electronics. The seven available contacts in the KAF bayonet are used differently for different types of AF lenses. The diagram here is that of the AF 50mm, f/1.4; AF 50mm, f/1.7; or AF 24-50mm, f/4 lenses.

bayonet, developed in 1975, into the fully functional KAF bayonet of 1987. Therefore it is possible for the existing Pentax user to decide on the new SFX, SFX_N and SF7 without having to forego any of the advantages of the old system, while the newcomer to Pentax may be assured of a well-tried system. The owner of an LX Super A, P-30, MX or K2 camera can use his SMC lenses on the SF7, SFX and SFX_N in all the exposure modes for which the lens is equipped, i.e. aperture priority, metered manual with the Pentax M lenses, and aperture priority, shutter speed priority and full program mode with the Pentax A

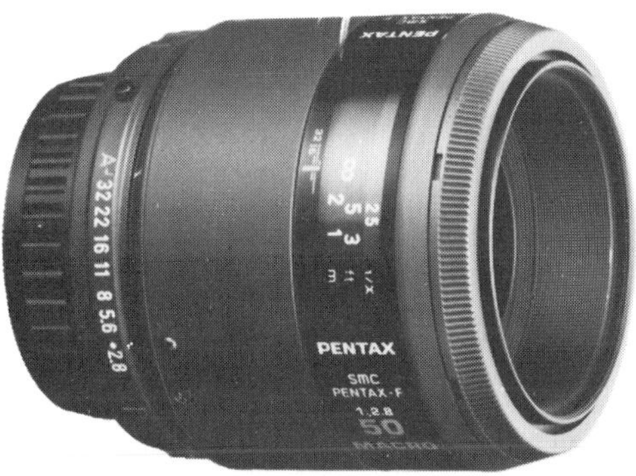

The AF 50mm, f/2.8 macro has floating elements to bring the reproduction scale down to 1:1 with excellent reproduction qualities throughout the whole focusing range.

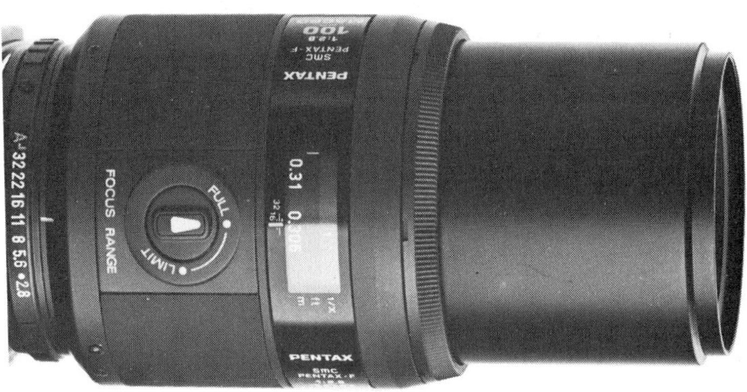

Because of its cleverly-designed focusing system, the AF 100mm, f/2.8 macro is only 4.5cm longer than the 50mm macro.

lenses. Focusing these lenses is done as usual by focusing ring, with the additional feature of the computer-assisted focusing control by LED indicators. Then there is the possibility of linking these "older" lenses to the SF7, SFX and SFX_N by a 1.7X SMC AF adapter. The use of the adapter allows full autofocus facility for all K and KA lenses and thus enhances the entire system.

If you are using a Pentax camera for the first time then the new system is by no means restricted to the, at first sight, somewhat limited range of AF lenses. For that special shot where you either do not need the autofocus function, or the appropriate lens is not yet available, you may choose from the varied range of SMC Pentax A lenses. Then there is the possibility of using any LX or Super A or P30 or even a ME camera as a second camera body because all of these are suitable for use with AF lenses, with the exposure programs for which the camera had been designed.

Fifteen AF Lenses: Angle of View from 84° to 4°

The Pentax AF system now offers 15 lenses. There are 8 AF lenses with fixed focal length: the AF 28mm,f/2.8, AF 50mm,f/1.4, AF 50mm,f/1.7, AF 50mm,f/2.8 macro, AF 100mm,f/2.8 macro, AF 135mm,f/2.8 IF, AF 300mm, f/4.5 ED/IF and the AF 600mm,f/4 ED/IF. These lenses represent a fairly comprehensive system for almost any photographic task.

Then there are the seven AF zoom lenses for the SF7, SFX and SFX_N which cover the focal length range from 24mm to 600mm, forming the second line of lenses for these cameras. Both types of lenses may be combined to

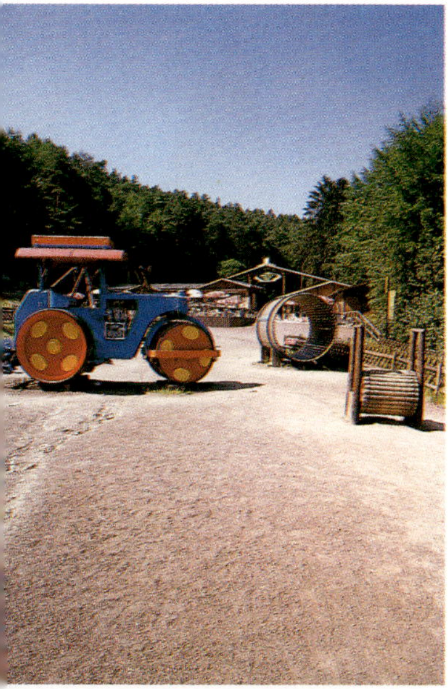
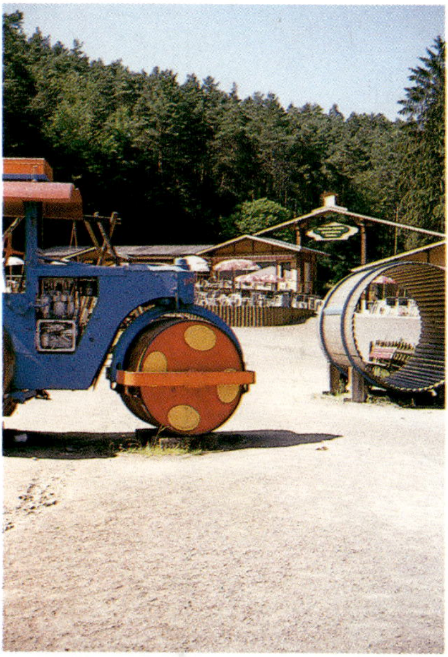
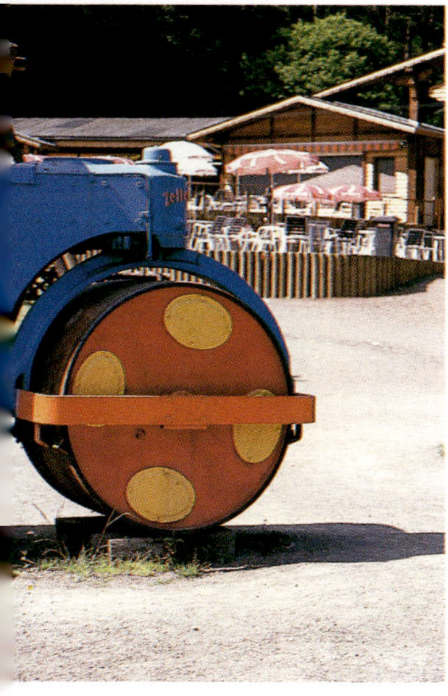
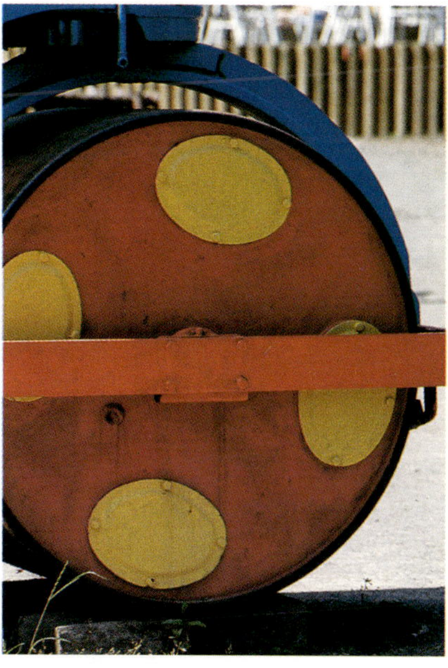

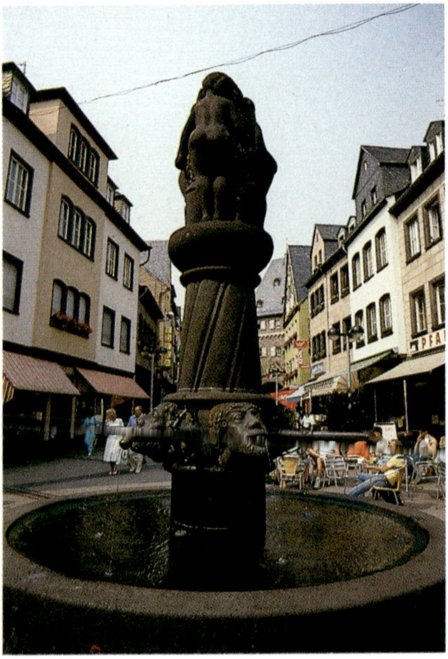

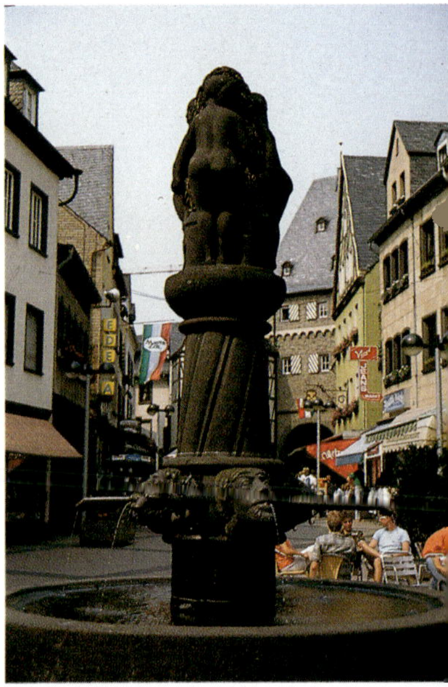

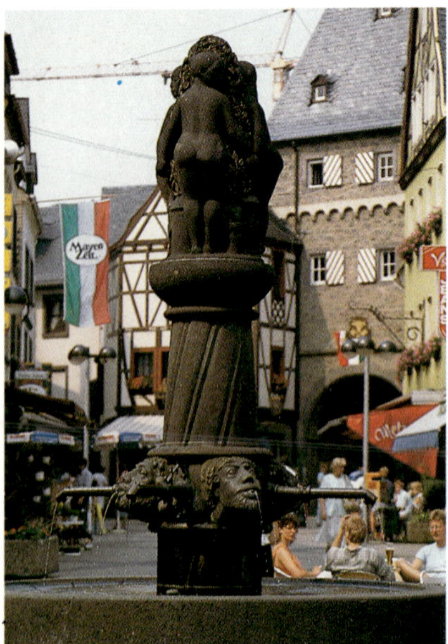
Mayen Zeit.

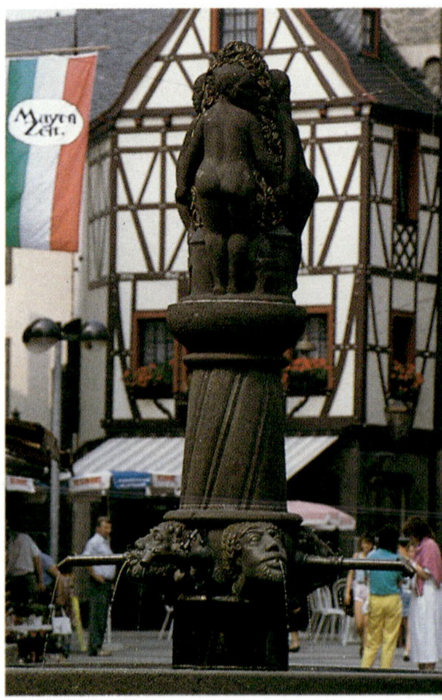
Mayen Zeit.

form the ideal equipment for individual requirements. For example, the AF fixed focal length AF 28mm, f/2.8 and the AF 100mm, f/2.8 macro, together with the wide-angle AF 24-50mm, f/4 zoom and the telephoto AF 70-210mm, f/4-5.6 zoom represents a comprehensive outfit for any conceivable situation. Those of you who swear by zoom lenses might decide on the three AF zoom lenses: 24-50mm, f/4 plus the 35-105mm, f/4-5.6 and the 70-210, f/4.5. These three variable length lenses, together with the AF 100mm, f/2.8 macro, the specialist for close-ups and large reproduction scales, complement each other and cover the whole range.

Always Young: The Standard Lens

The two standard AF lenses, the 50mm, f/1.4 and the 50mm, f/1.7 are the classical and still very popular lenses as an initial choice for the Pentax SF7, SFX or SFX_N. At the moment these are the fastest of the AF lenses. Most photographers would consider adding a standard lens to their range for the sake of high speed; even those who wish to explore their photographic world mainly by a range of zoom lenses.

The reason why a 50mm lens is called a standard lens is quite simple. If the focal length of a lens is as long as the diagonal of the negative format it will depict a 53° angle of view. This is a little larger than the angle of view with sharp vision of the human eye, which lies somewhere between 45-50°, depending on the individual. We therefore consider pictures taken with a standard lens as "normal". Naturally this only applies if the whole negative has been enlarged or the whole slide has been projected.

Variations in perspective: The focal length determines the angle of view, the distance to the main subject determines its size in the picture – only a change in subject distance will alter the proportions of foreground and background.
Photo: Richard Hünecke

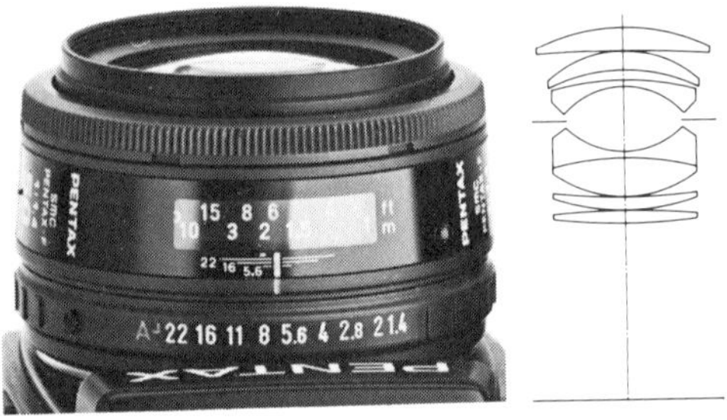

The AF 50mm, f/1.4 lens offers high speed and excellent reproduction quality at a modest price.

The diagonal of the 24x36mm negative format is actually 43.3mm, but 50mm was adopted as the focal length of the standard lens 60 years ago as giving a more natural angle of view. This was fortunate because it now allows greater structural freedom and gives room for the fold-away mirror that needs to be accommodated behind the lens. These dimensions result in an angle of view of 47°.

The AF 50mm, f/1.4 has the same specifications as the 50mm, f/1.7 apart from the extra half-stop of lens speed. Both lenses offer excellent reproduction qualities such as sharpness, good contrast, resolution, high speed and uniform illumination of the entire picture area, at a reasonable price. The straightforward, true-to-reality character of these lenses makes them extremely easy to use. Later we come to appreciate the standard lens for its suitability for photo reportage without the need for distorted interpretations by unusual perspective. For the available-light photographer the standard lens is an invaluable tool to be carried with him at any time. It can be used in situations where a flashgun is not welcome or its use would destroy the intimate mood of the scene. If you load your camera with one of the new fast high resolution ISO 1600/33° films, you can get excellent pictures even in very low light. However, if the AF 35-70mm, f/3.5-4.5 zoom is the only lens handy at the time, even at its largest aperture of f/3.5 at 35mm, being 2½ stops slower than the standard lens, you will be forced to use shutter speeds of ½ to 1 sec., which is not feasible for hand-held shots.

Another variation of the 50mm standard focal length is represented by the AF 50mm, f/2.8 macro lens. Although 1½ aperture stops slower than the other two 50mm lenses, it can be focused down to 20cm, with a reproduction scale of 1:1. Furthermore, its reproduction qualities are excellent, particularly in the close range.

A Wider Angle to Capture More of the Subject

It makes no difference whether you use the Pentax AF 28mm, f/2.8 or select the shortest focal length on the AF 24-50mm, f/4 zoom, the rules for the use and application of a wide-angle lens are the same. The special characteristics of the wide-angle lens, particularly noticeable with the 24mm setting on the zoom, the shortest AF focal length for the SFX, SFX_N and SF7 available, can be appreciated when looking through the viewfinder. The lens captures a large section of the subject space in the 75° angle of view and even more so in the 84° angle of view. You need to move really close to the subject. If you think you are close enough, advance another three steps, otherwise an endless foreground leads up to a main subject that appears small and insignificant, seeming almost to merge into the far-away background. Photographing with a wide-angle lens implies the correct assessment of relative size of the subjects in the fore- and background, i.e. knowing how they will be represented by the lens. A piece of timber on the shore, weathered by wind and waves, over-large in the foreground, sets the right accent for spatial depth of the sea behind it. Use aperture priority and preselect a small aperture for as large a depth of field as possible (but don't forget to check the shutter speed for shake-free shots).

With the wide-angle lens you can shoot tall buildings at an oblique angle for a dramatic effect. The obliquely distorted proportions of a newspaper stand in front of the glass facade of a modern office block could be an effective composition – the strict, rectangular outlines are distorted to trapezoid shapes, seemingly falling backwards. If you cannot avoid an oblique shooting angle, make the most of it; move as close as possible to the subject and take the steepest shooting angle possible. Now you will be able to capture the glass-concrete facade rising steeply away into the sky. The clouds sailing by as reflections in the sleek facade add a special abstract effect. In such compositions it is advisable to keep the horizontal lines of the facade parallel to the upper and lower edges of the picture. It looks better if the upright sides appear to be rising at an equal angle on both sides of the picture.

Bright sky outlining slim architecture. This is the typical subject where the **ML** button is essential. **PROCES** will compensate to a certain extent for the over-bright sky but it may not be sufficient. You can never be sure how it will turn out and when the picture comes back from the lab it will be too late to repeat the shot. Luck will play a large part in whether the building is shown in its correct luminosity and colour. The wise photographer follows the **PROCES** exposure by two or three extra ones, using spot metering to measure a very dark section of the structure, followed by a less dark and then a bright part of the building. If you change over to metered manual mode, then spot metering will always be activated. This has the advantage that after adjusting the exposure you do not have to hold the **ML** button but can concentrate fully on arranging the framing of the subject. However, do not store the setting for too long, the lighting could change; if a cloud moves across the sun the exposure will be incorrect.

Photographing with a wide-angle lens means having to arrange the foreground. To keep a space of five metres free of any object could give the impression of a wide open empty space. How attractive this will look depends on the way you arrange it, so that it presents a suitable contrast to the main subject, without overshadowing it. An old plant pot in the garden, a basket of fruit in the market, a cast iron lantern in a street scene, the sleek bumper of a limousine in a run-down back street – all to fill the foreground, that's what is important!

The moderate wide-angle setting of 35mm has to be treated in a similar fashion, only the effects are not so pronounced. Three of the seven AF zoom lenses start with this focal length and the 35mm focal length has become the modern version of the standard lens for many people. They find that, compared with the 50mm lens, the 35mm images have a more dynamic effect. It also favours the quick, close-in snapshot.

Viewing Distant Things

Turning the zoom ring of the AF 35-70mm, f/3.5-4.5 to its longest setting gives you a taste of how the longer focal lengths bridge distances and bring a small subject large into the frame. Pentax offer fixed focal length AF telephoto lenses in the traditional focal lengths of 100mm, 135mm, 300mm and 600mm. This focal length range presents clear differences in the sections that are embraced of the subject space and noticeable variations in perspective, but only if you also change your shooting position together with the lens. If you wish to cover this range you might also consider that the range of 70 - 600mm can be covered by just two AF zoom lenses, namely the AF 70-210mm, f/4-5.6 and the AF 250-600mm, f/5.6. The small gap of 40mm between 210 and 250mm, representing two degrees of angle of view, can be ignored. However, this fascination with long focal lengths costs a lot in both weight and money.

The AF 70-210mm,f/4-5.6 zoom is now the most popular moderate telephoto zoom covering the popular and useful focal length of 135mm and giving you a taste of the super-telephoto range at the longest setting. The nearest focusing distance of this lens is 1.1m, giving a reproduction scale of 1:4 at the 210mm setting. This leaves us with just one more wish to make this the ideal lens for almost every situation; why not construct a 70-210mm zoom at reasonable cost, but with one more aperture stop, to be able to use it in situations where a large aperture would be necessary?

Regardless of whether you use a fixed focal length lens or a zoom to isolate a small section of the subject, the basic principle remains unchanged; the longer the focal length, the smaller the section, the closer the background appears to crowd in on the subject, the depth of field becomes narrower and shutter speeds have to be faster for safe hand-held shots. The long focal lengths are creative tools of a very special kind.

The Moderate Telephoto Lens: By moderate we mean focal lengths around 85 to 100mm. In the Pentax AF range this is covered by the longest focal length setting of the AF 28-80mm zoom and, more comprehensively, by the AF 35-105mm. Many photographers consider either one of these their universal lens, as they are ideal for landscape and portraiture, as well as being well-suited for small sections of landscapes, architectural details, for the whole spectrum of still-life and close-up photography and for people at work and play. These focal lengths allow any unnecessary detail to be excluded from the frame, without being too restrictive. Using a moderate telephoto lens is almost as easy as handling a standard 50mm lens.

Amongst the fixed focal length lenses in the Pentax AF range we find only one lens that fills the bill. Although the choice is restricted to one lens only, it is a real beauty; the AF 100mm,f/2.8 macro! Its long helicoid gear may be focused down to a 30cm subject distance, giving a reproduction scale of 1:1. This requires a little less than one revolution of the focusing ring and extends the tube by only 4.5cm. The constraints on optical design which meant that a lens could only be corrected for a relatively small reproduction range, within which it would produce its best image quality that deteriorated rapidly beyond these limits, have been overcome by the Asahi designers. Behind the gauss group of 6 basic elements they have installed another group of 3 elements. This corrective group shifts its position during focusing so that its distance to the film plane is always kept constant. This ensures that excellent image quality is maintained throughout the entire focusing range, from infinity down to the 1:1 reproduction ratio.

This lens can be considered an ideal all-rounder, suitable for landscapes, portraiture, still-life, close-up and macro photography. The small switch on the mount of the lens divides the setting range of the lens between infinity to a reproduction scale of 1:4 and the close-up range from 1:3 down to 1:1.

Typical Telephoto Lenses: The classical representative of this focal length is the 135mm lens and Pentax offer this focal length in the form of the AF 135mm, f/2.8. The upper limit of this focal length range of 200mm, or a little above, can be covered by the AF 70-210mm, f/4-5.6. Both of these lenses are typical of the longer focal lengths by compressing the spatial depth and bringing the far away background closer to the main subject. The term "depth of field" takes on new meanings with a long focus lens. The depth of field shrinks considerably, even for medium distances and small apertures, but the main subject will be set against a blurred back- and foreground. It is particularly important that the main subject is in sharp focus – but this is no problem for the AF function of the Pentax SF cameras. Even manual focusing is no problem, if you are looking for a 200mm lens and decide to use the SMC 200mm, f/2.8 A lens, or the SMC 200mm, f/4 ED macro A lens that is capable of a reproduction ratio of 1:1, as Pentax has not brought out similar models in the AF version. Do not forget to check the shutter speed in the viewfinder. For lenses of focal lengths between 135 and 200mm the shutter speed should not be slower than 1/250 sec. If you also support your camera on a tripod, even though the shutter speed is within safe limits, you are a wise person. Despite the excellent qualities of the Pentax lenses the picture will be blurred if the camera moves by even the smallest amount. If the light gets low and you did not bring your tripod, open up the aperture as far as possible to get as fast a shutter speed as possible. The resulting shallow depth of field will definitely be better than a blurred shot. A slightly greater depth of field would not make up for the blurred outlines and if you focus precisely on the subject, the shallow depth of field is usually very attractive, although it is not ideal for every subject.

The AF 135mm, f/2.8 can be focused down to 70cm and shows a subject, size 15x10cm, at a reproduction ratio of 1:4.

Special Ingredient: ED Glass: The extremely expensive ED glasses were designed for lenses of the highest quality; it means that the elements have very low dispersion to correct reproduction errors that cannot be rectified in any other way. Fast lenses with long focal lengths – for a 300mm focal length lens an initial opening of f/4.5 is deemed very fast – are more liable to second-order colour aberrations than lenses with short focal lengths. This means they will project coloured fringes around otherwise quite clearly defined areas making sharp outlines unsharp. Eliminating this colour aberration may be likened to a rebellion against a natural law and can only be achieved by using very expensive glasses, which possess, apart from a very high refractive index, low dispersion. Pentax offer three AF lenses with these ED glasses for almost aberration-free pictures with high resolution, excellent contrast and optimum sharpness. These are the AF 300mm, f/4.5 EF/IF, the AF 600mm, f/4.6 ED/IF, and the AF zoom 250-600, f/5.6 ED.

IF stands for internal focusing. This means that only one element group is moved and not the entire optical system. This implies several advantages for the AF 300mm, f/4.5 EF/IF; the time taken to focus from infinity to the 2m close-up limit is 0.8 sec. The lens does not change its length and so the centre of gravity is not shifted during focusing resulting in safer handling which is particularly important for hand-held shooting, provided the lens is not too heavy.

The AF 300mm, f/4.5 ED/IF weighs 880g and measures only 160mm. But don't get carried away by the fact it seems to lend itself to hand-held shooting. A lens of this focal length is not safe for shutter speeds slower than 1/250 sec. but 1/500 sec. is really the safer limit. If circumstances demand a slower shutter speed you will have to use a tripod. To balance the camera/lens combination, attach the lens to the tripod and not the camera. The tripod socket on the lens is not particularly beautiful but it is large and solidly built and forms an excellent handgrip. The AF 300mm, f/4.5 ED/IF, being a typical super-telephoto lens, compresses the spatial depth in characteristic fashion and brings the distant background closer to the main subject. The perspective, familiar from the shorter focal lengths, is absent from shots taken of distant subjects with these long focal length lenses. Depth of field is another factor that has to be revised, it gets narrower the closer the focusing distance. It is important to focus precisely on the subject; the qualities of the lens will help you to obtain good results and to lift the main subject against an unsharp fore- and background. The internal focusing distance can provide a close-up shooting distance of 2m, for a 22x15cm subject area – the depth of field with an aperture of f/11 will be measurable; it will be only 1cm! But the perspective and the effect of this extremely small depth of field for such a close-up is much more striking than with the AF 50mm, f/1.7 from a distance of 45cm.. The fast super-telephoto AF 600mm, f/4 ED/IF doubles everything that has been said about the AF 300mm, f/4.5 ED/IF – twice the focal length and perhaps twice the excitement – but it also doubles the requirements for the photographer's skills and the shooting conditions. This lens is definitely the expert in wild-life and sports photography, and also for the dramatic view of a bland landscape. This lens is quite often used under extreme environmental conditions and the precious front element is therefore protected by a colourless filter. In the lens tube is a compartment for the six specially designed correction and

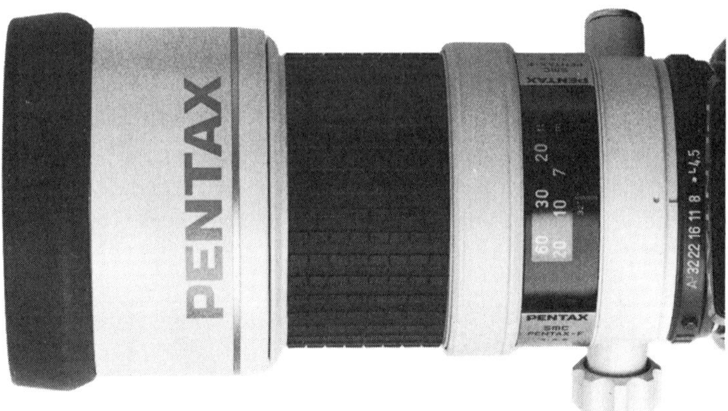

A very handy and perfectly balanced telephoto lens, the AF 300mm, f/4.5 ED/IF, for the long distance shot.

colour filters. These belong to the lens and are part of it. The 600mm ED/IF weighs a hefty 6830g and you will also need at all times a very strong tripod.

The AF 250-600mm, f/5.6 ED zoom is comparable in its specifications to the 600mm ED/IF. This lens may be counted amongst the very best in optical engineering, combining almost everything that can be expected of a powerful zoom lens with regard to optical and structural design at a price that is still reasonable. This lens does not need the refinement of internal focusing as it avails itself of a different construction favoured for zoom lenses. In order to increase focusing speed it has, similar to the AF 600mm, f/4, a focus lock for limiting the focusing movement to certain ranges.

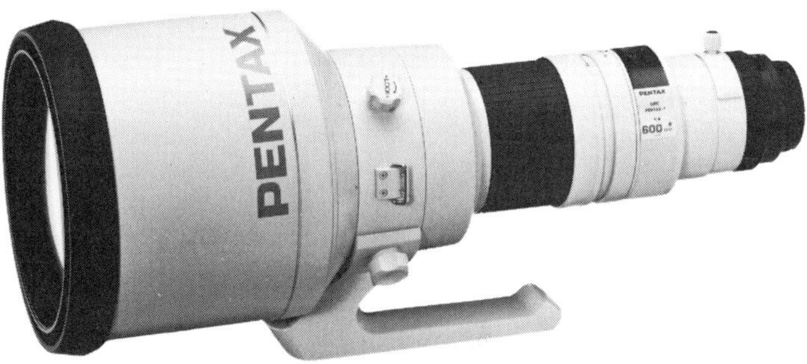

The very fast AF 600, f/4 ED/IF super-telephoto with excellent reproduction qualities for the wild-life and sports photographer.

Zoom Lenses for Continuous Variation of Angle of View

The AF 250-600mm, f/5.6 ED zoom is in a class of its own. The six other AF zooms for the Pentax SF cameras cover a focal length range of 24mm to 210mm to form a complete system, independent of the fixed focal length lenses. These zoom lenses cover exactly the range where most photographic action takes place. Pentax have also included two macro lenses for the Pentax AF system and the SF photographer will therefore hardly have to look in the SMC A range of lenses to find a specific fixed focal length lens to complement his range of AF zoom lenses. He will most likely choose one of the fixed focal length lenses for special assignments, such as available light photography, or a super wide-angle lens for the all-embracing view. The six zooms in the focal length range 24mm to 210mm, which could also be covered by four fixed focal length lenses, will raise the question as to which combination of lenses will be the best for the individual photographer. If it is important to cover a large range of focal lengths the AF 70-210mm, f/4-5.6 zoom could be one of the partners of a pair of zoom lenses. This lens can be focused down to 1.1m. At a focal length setting of 70mm the reproduction scale is 1:12, which increases continuously to 1:4 by turning the zoom ring to the 210mm focal length, which will show a 15x10cm small subject full-frame in the negative.

This zoom lens may be complemented by the AF 35-70mm, f/3.5-4.5 zoom. This pair of zooms is doubtless a most useful combination as it covers the entire popular focal length range with only two lenses. The angle of view covered starts on the wide side with 63° and ends at just 12° on the narrow side. To complement these two lenses, or perhaps only the long telephoto zoom lens in the wide-angle range, you might choose the wide-angle AF 24-50mm, f/4 zoom. This extends the angle of view covered down to 84° on the wide side. The 24mm wide-angle lens has now almost become part of the standard equipment of most photographers. The AF 24-50mm, f/4 zoom is a great favourite amongst many dedicated photographers. It is very useful as a partner for the 70-210mm, f/4-5.6 telephoto zoom lens. The small gap from 47°, for the 50mm, to 34.5°, for the 70mm setting of the long telephoto lens, is generally easily covered by going a few feet closer or further away from the subject.

If you are not too concerned about the longer focal length range you may be very well served by the AF 35-135mm, f/3.5-4.5 zoom. This one lens covers the popular focal length range in SLR photography with an angle of

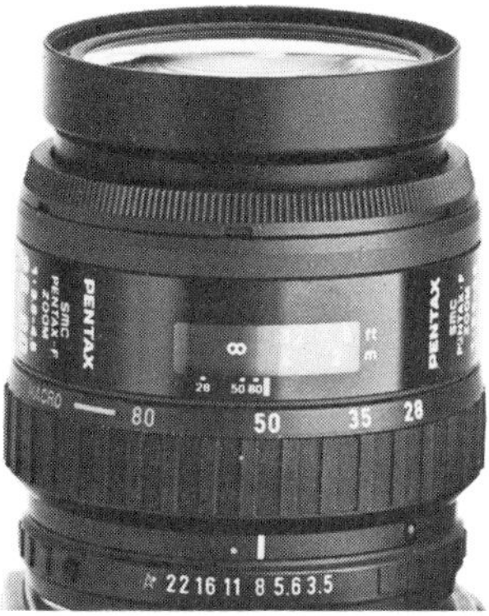

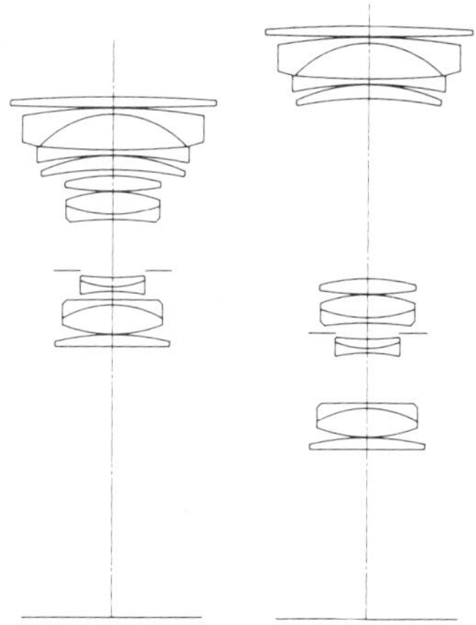

The compact and handy AF 28-80mm, f/3.5-4.5 zoom is an excellent partner to carry on your camera when casually exploring your surroundings.

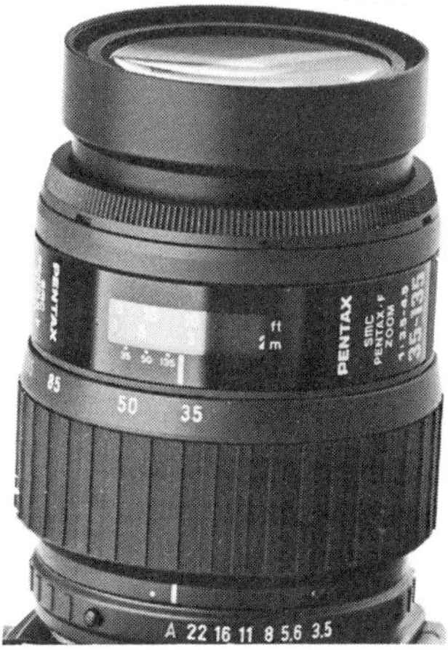

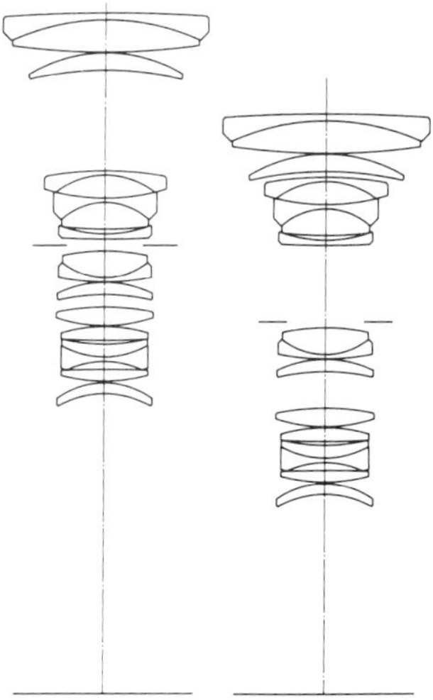

The classic focal lengths of SLR photography combined here in one lens, the AF 35-135mm f/3.5-4.5 zoom.

view of 63° to 18°. You could later complement this zoom with a wide-angle zoom and the longer telephoto zoom. This means that some focal lengths in the middle of the range will be duplicated but this need not necessarily be a disadvantage. On the contrary, carrying the 35-135mm as a "standard" lens on your camera will equip you for a great variety of subjects and situations without having to change the lens. A further advantage is that the reproduction scale at the 135mm setting in the close range is 1:4.

The fast standard lens is still the best start for most photographers building up a comprehensive system. However, if you ask the user of a standard lens how often he really uses the largest aperture setting of f/1.4 or f/1.7, the answer will be most surprising; "very rarely"! If, on the other hand, you take the 35-70mm,f/3.5-4.5 zoom as your "standard" lens, or its slightly longer focal range partner, the AF 28-80mm,f/3.5-4.5, you will experience from the very first moment the total delights of SLR photography; the precise and free composition of a picture framed in the viewfinder taken from a suitable and convenient shooting position. The AF 35-70mm f/3.5-4.5 is only a little larger and heavier and not much more expensive than the standard AF 50mm,f/1.4. The difference between the standard lens and the AF 28-80mm, f/3.5-4.5, on the other hand, having an appreciably larger focal length range, is more noticeable. If, later on, you are drawn towards scenes at dusk, then you can complement your range of lenses with the AF 50mm,f/1.4, or any other suitable fast fixed focal length lens that will cover your requirements with respect to angle of view and speed.

Autofocus technology dictates that zoom lenses must be constructed with two rings. The focal length is adjusted by a rotating ring and not by a sliding sleeve, focusing being done by a separate ring. This is slower than the combined zoom/focusing adjustment by a single sliding sleeve but I prefer this construction for various reasons. Firstly it is easy to handle and secondly, it will retain the setting even if you are shooting at an oblique angle with the camera screwed to the tripod.

The SMC-AF Adapter 1.7X

At a quick glance you might confuse it with one of the still quite popular teleconverters. These are used between the camera and the lens to extend the focal length of the lens by a factor of 2 or more, but also reducing the speed and increasing all aperture values by the same factor. The disadvantage is that any aberrations or other faults of even the best lens are increased by the same factor. This is exactly the point why universal converters that are manufactured to fit any lens from Pentax to Zeiss, have their weaknesses. It pays to be consistent; after all, you have spent a fair amount of money on your Pentax outfit, so why spoil it by not investing in the specifically-designed converter for the Pentax system to get the best possible results that will do your lenses justice.

The AF adapter 1.7X has only six electrical contacts in the front face of its bayonet. This corresponds to the KA system

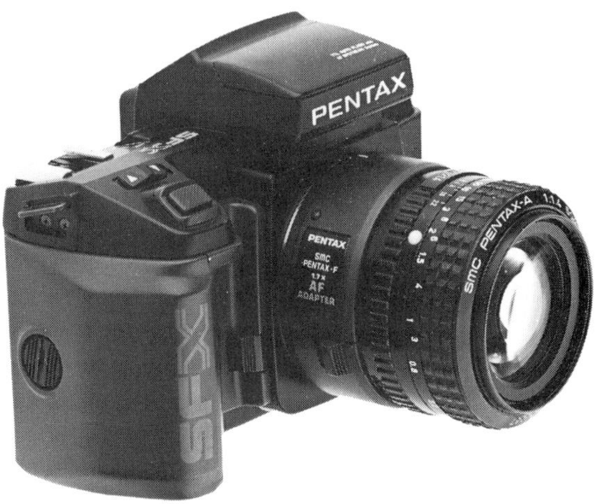

The AF Adapter 1.7X serves as an adapter for automatic focusing and at the same time extends the focal length of the lens by a factor of 1.7. A lens with KA or K bayonet has to have a maximum aperture of at least f/2.8 to provide sufficient speed.

for the lens to be attached. At the rear face, which is to be attached to the SFX, there are seven contacts, together with the typical AF coupling. Turning this coupling very carefully with a small screwdriver, the group of elements within will move by about 5mm. The autofocus motor will drive these elements and consequently focus the attached A-lens within a limited distance range. The lens system in an intermediate ring has the same effect as a converter, and the AF converter not only focuses the lens, it also increases the focal length of the lens and, by necessity, reduces the lens speed, each by a factor of 1.7. For this reason you have to choose a lens with a speed of at least f/2.8 to allow the CCD image sensor to take meaningful readings. This requirement precludes the slower lenses from use with the AF adapter 1.7X. The following Pentax A lenses are suitable:

These SMC-A lenses	give these combinations
16mm,f/2.8 Fisheye	27mm,f/4.8
20mm,f/2.8	34mm,f/4.8
24mm,f/2.8	41mm,f/4.8
28mm,f/2.0	47mm,f/3.4
28mm,f/2.8	47mm,f/4.8
35mm,f/2.0	60mm,f/3.4
35mm,f/2.8	60mm,f/4.8
50mm,f/1.2	85mm,f/2.0
50mm,f/1.4	85mm,f/2.4
50mm,f/1.7	85mm,f/2.9
50mm,f/2.0	85mm,f/3.4
85mm,f/1.4	144mm,f/2.4
100mm,f/2.8	170mm,f/4.8
135mm,f/1.8	230mm,f/3.1
135mm,f/2.8	230mm,f/4.8

Hunting for your macro subject with a hand-held camera is a joy with the SFX in shutter speed priority and AF-SERVO modes. Preselect at least 1/125 second and allow the aperture to adapt to the prevailing lighting conditions. AF 100mm, f/2.8 Macro. Photo: Richard Hünecke

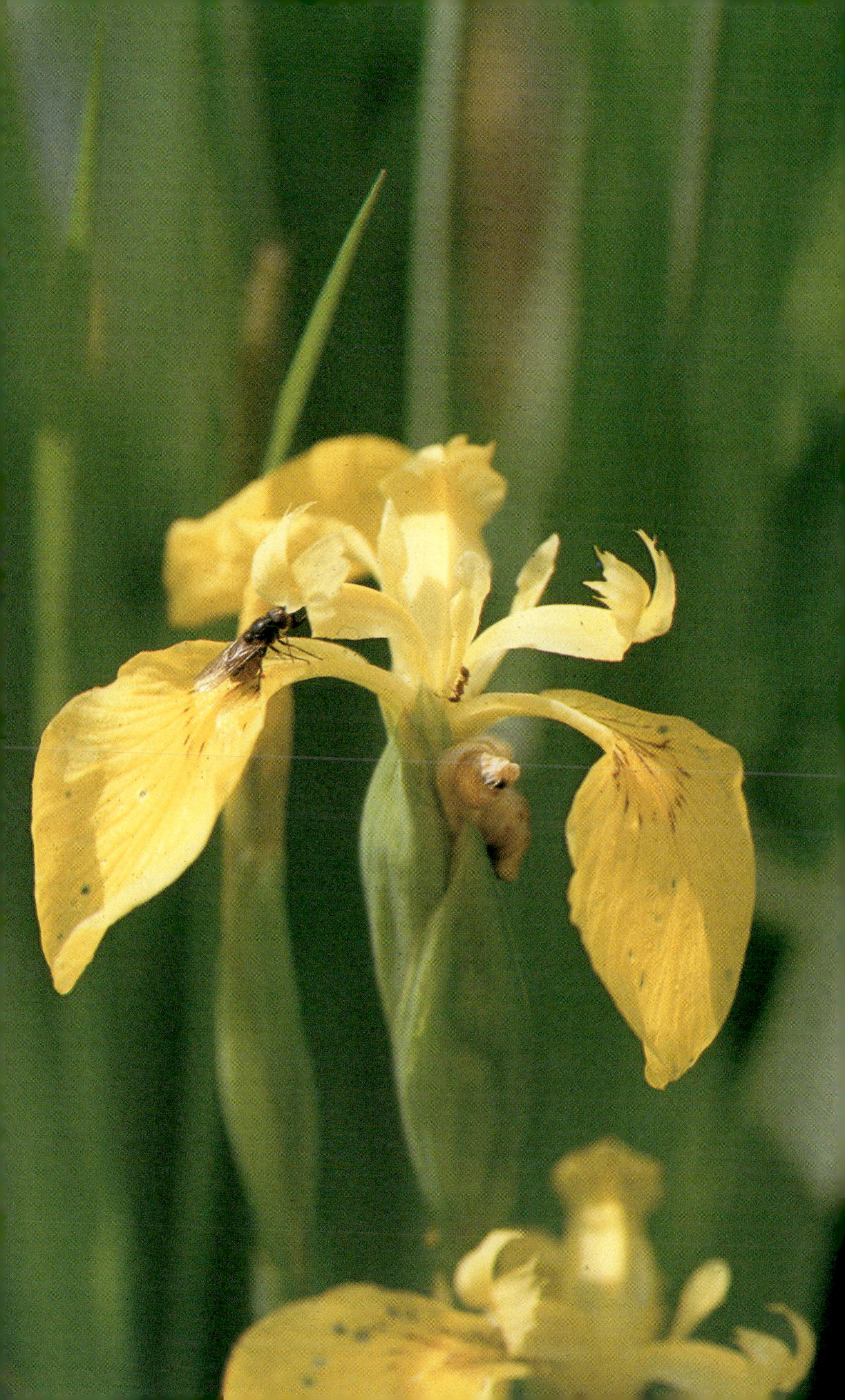

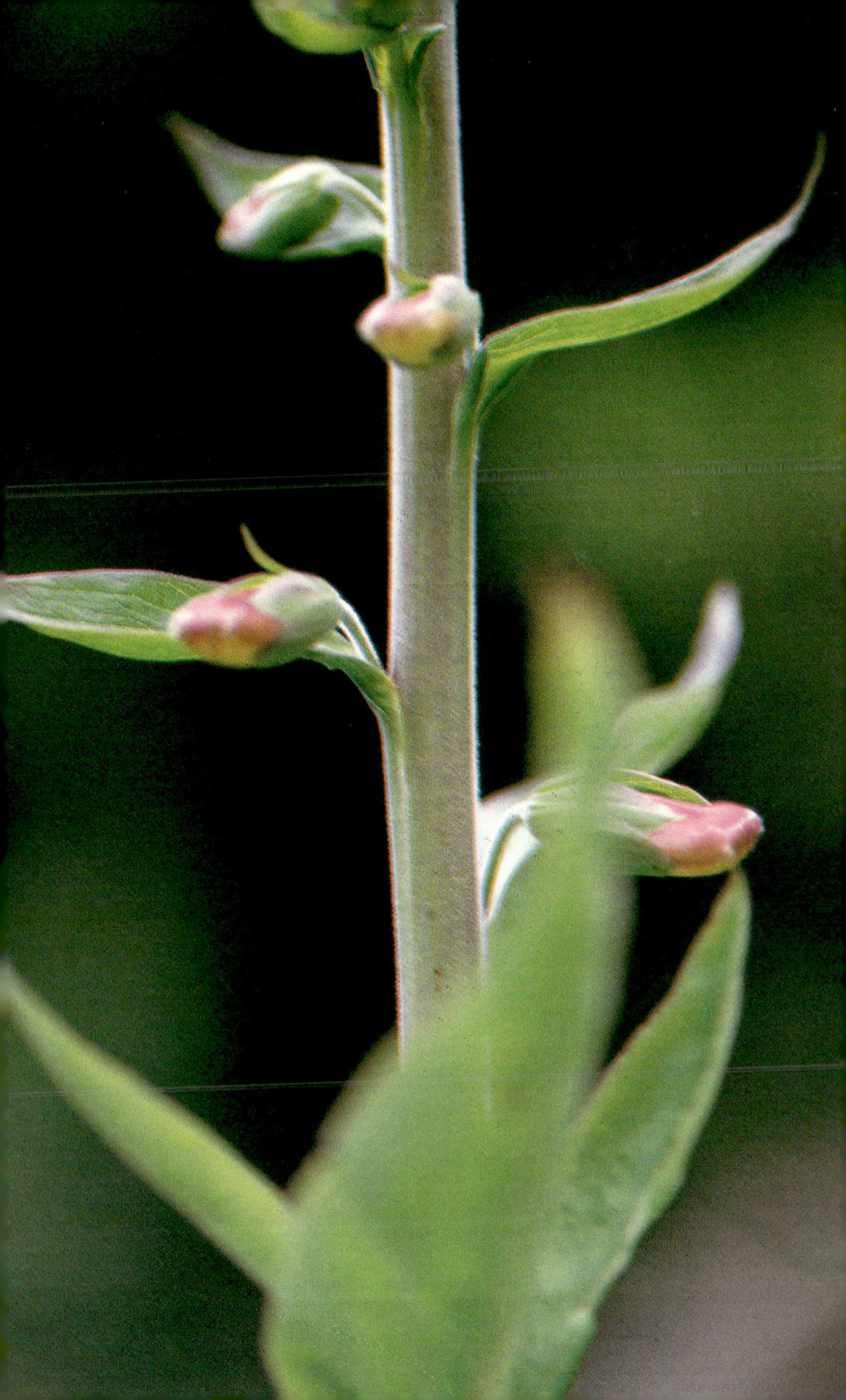

These SMC-A lenses	give these combinations
200mm,f/2.8 ED	340mm,f/4.8
300mm,f/2.8 ED/IF	510mm,f/4.8
400mm,f/2.8 ED/IF	680mm,f/4.8
35-105mm,f/3.5 Zoom without macro range	60-179mm,f/6.0

Attach the AF adapter to the SFX, then attach the Pentax A-lens to the adapter. Select a shooting mode as usual and also the focusing mode, lift the SFX to your eye and lightly press the release. All camera functions will operate as usual, as if an AF lens was attached. With one exception though: the rather short focusing distance of only 5mm is not sufficient to focus the lens through its entire focusing range – except for very short focal length lenses. You will therefore have to roughly pre-focus the lens, the exact focusing being performed by the autofocus system when the release is pressed. The two actions can be easily and quickly performed and focusing will always be faster this way than with manual focusing. The specified focusing time of 0.3 seconds applies to the 5mm focusing path of the AF adapter, not to the adjustment of the attached lens from infinity to close-up. Again, the condition: no focus – no picture applies in the SINGLE shooting mode just as for the AF lens. As far as the autofocus function is concerned, it does not matter whether you attach a Pentax A-lens to the AF adapter, or a Pentax M or K lens. However, not all the possible program options offered by the SFX can be utilised with these lenses, only the aperture priority mode and the metered manual shooting mode will be possible. The operating conditions are thus similar to those of a Pentax LX or ME Super, with the addition of an electronic/manual focusing aid.

The 210mm focal length setting brings this shot easily into the frame, and at sufficient distance to avoid disturbing the subject; it allows the background to dissolve into an attractive blur. AF 70-210mm Zoom.

Photo: Richard Hünecke

But if you are taking out an old Takumar lens with M-42 thread from the bottom of your gadget bag and try to screw this, via the Pentax M42/K adapter to the SMC-AF adapter, then you will have come across the limits of system compatability. The AF adapter will no longer function as an autofocus adapter, only as a teleconverter. The focusing indicator LED also will not respond and you will have to focus visually by focusing screen. From all the possible exposure modes the only available ones that will function with this lens will be the working aperture mode and the simple metered manual mode, as well as exposure metering with working aperture.

The SMC Pentax Shift 28mm.f/3.5 lens is not suitable for the AF system via the AF adapter either. The shift functions cannot be utilized because the obliquely shifted light beam cannot be transmitted through the optical system of the adapter.

A Heart for Oldies

The Pentax SFX accepts any Pentax lens with K or KA bayonet. Naturally, these lenses will have to be focused manually. The focus-assist facility will remain active when using a lens from this range. The red LEDs indicate by the direction of the arrow in which direction the focusing ring should be turned to obtain perfect focus. If the red arrows are replaced by the green hexagon, then the K- or KA lens is properly focused on the subject outlined within the focusing field at the centre of the viewfinder. Should you wish to focus on another detail, not at the centre of the viewfinder, then you may simply disregard the LED indicators.

Lenses with a KA bayonet can be used in all the available shooting modes of the SFX as long as the lens is designed for it. Here too, when setting the aperture ring to manual, you change from program mode or shutter speed priority to aperture priority. In TTL flash mode and in automatic flash

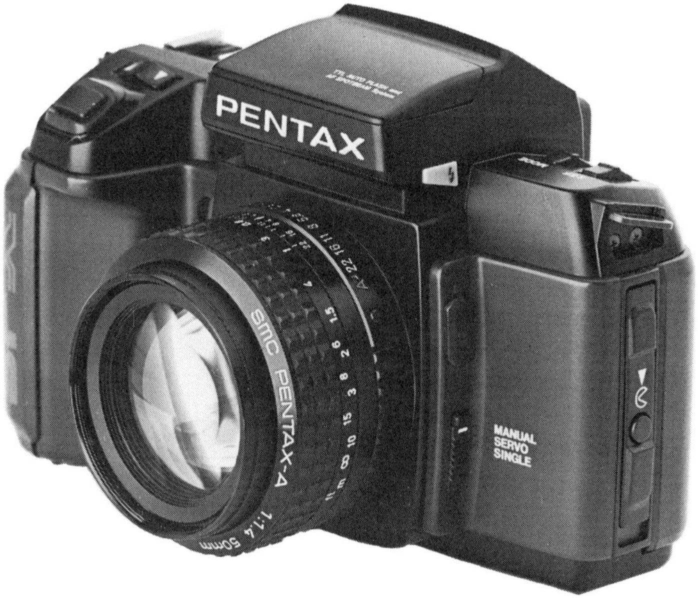

The SMĈ-A lens fits as perfectly on the SFX as it does on a Super A or LX Pentax camera.

mode the flashgun attached, either directly to the hot shoe or via a TTL synchronization cable, will determine the function of the combination with the camera. Naturally, Pentax lenses with the simple K-bayonet can only be used in aperture mode and metered manual mode. The TTL controlled flashgun may now only be controlled by the appropriately programmed flashgun and by the manually-selected aperture on the K-lens.

Intermediate conclusion: friends of the Pentax system who wish to extend their existing equipment of, say, a Pentax LX, Super-A, MX, P-30 or ME-Super camera and a range of K- or KA lenses, by trying the SFX together with perhaps just one AF lens, need not completely re-think their whole equipment concept, nor all the well-tried combinations. On the other hand it is to be expected that the continued logic of the Pentax systems will allow the inclusion of future lenses within the SFX

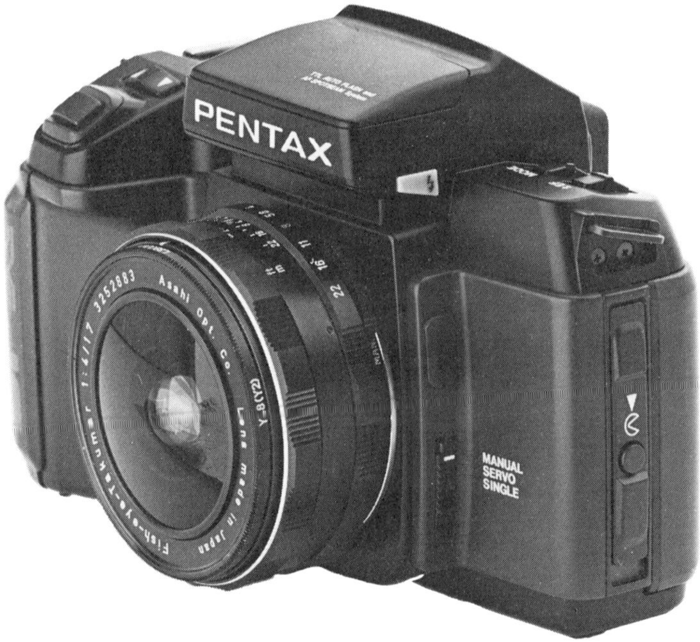

The M42/K Adapter makes it possible for the old Fisheye-Takumar to fit onto the SFX. This adapter hides unnoticed in the KAF bayonet and it is possible to focus this and any other M42 bayonet lens from infinity to the close-up limit.

system. For example, we can look forward to the Soft 85mm,f/2.2 lens, the specialist lens for the romantic look, the soft rendition of romantic landscapes, and ancient ruins. Or the Super Tele 600mm,f/5.6 ED/IF lens to bring the heraldic emblem at the top of the tower into full frame for close inspection. Or the Super Wide-angle 15mm,f/3.5 lens for space-embracing effects never seen with the naked eye. One hint on using the latter: hold the camera absolutely straight, otherwise you end up with very ugly distortions of the architectural lines. And pay great attention to the space close to the camera, unless you are after a feeling of emptiness; you have to fill this space with suitable objects: a vase of flowers, the reflection of the main subject in a puddle, the picturesque lines of an old horse-drawn vehicle. Such objects in the foreground also serve to take the viewer's eyes from the foreground and lead them to the actual subject in the background. If you think you are already close enough to the subject, move a little closer; the enormous 111° angle of view of the 15mm lens gives immense coverage.

The very popular SMC Shift 28mm,f/3.5 can easily be used with the SFX. You focus before you apply the shift, either by visual check on the focusing screen or by the focus-assist facility. The Shift lens has only a simple aperture (no automatic diaphragm) therefore it has to be used in working aperture mode or metered manual mode. The experienced photographer knows that the best possible result for the wide-angle shot is guaranteed if you take a series of exposures.

Even an old Fisheye Takumar can be used provided you attach it via the M42/K-adapter. Naturally it will have to be focused manually; the focus has to be checked on the focusing screen and the choice of exposure modes is restricted to working aperture priority and metered manual mode.

So this evolution of the Pentax system into the autofocus era has been defined by Pentax as a development that keeps in mind the photographer who uses existing equipment; therefore it is not completely revolutionary. This development is a forward-thinking continuity of the system.

Small Things Made Large in a Picture

Look at small things around you: an insect, the shavings of the three coloured pencils left by the pencil sharpener on the table, any ordinary object that you can imagine as a large and impressive poster-sized print. You point your Pentax at the small item and find that the focusing range stops before you get close enough for a frame-filling view of the small object you wish to depict. A 75cm close-up used to be the limit for the 50mm standard lens corresponding to a reproduction scale of 1:12. Modern developments have brought this close-up limit to the currently accepted 45cm. Does this mean that the fascinating realm of close-up photography starts at this point? Yes and no! There is one SLR camera in existence which has a standard lens with helical focusing that allows a close-up limit of 30cm! Does this mean then that macro photography starts at 29.5cm? On the other hand there is the Pentax AF 300mm,f/4.5 ED/IF lens that represents an object at 200cm distance larger on film than the Pentax standard AF 50mm,f/1.7 from 45cm shooting distance.

What then is the definition of macro photography? The overriding definition is the reproduction scale! This is the relationship between the size of the object in front of the lens and the size of the object on film. This is usually smaller, but it can also be larger than the original. A reproduction scale 1:5 means that the object is represented at one fifth the actual size in the negative. Reproduction scale 2:1 means that the image on the film is twice the size of the object. Reproduction scale is also defined by the ratio of the distance to the object - i.e. the distance of the subject to the lens – to the distance of the

Using the light reflected from a white wall and the focal length set at 210mm on the AF 70-210mm lens were the ingredients in this close-up. The SFX was set to shutter speed priority, and the exposure control could provide the widest aperture setting for the preselected $^{1}/_{125}$ second. Photo: Richard Hünecke

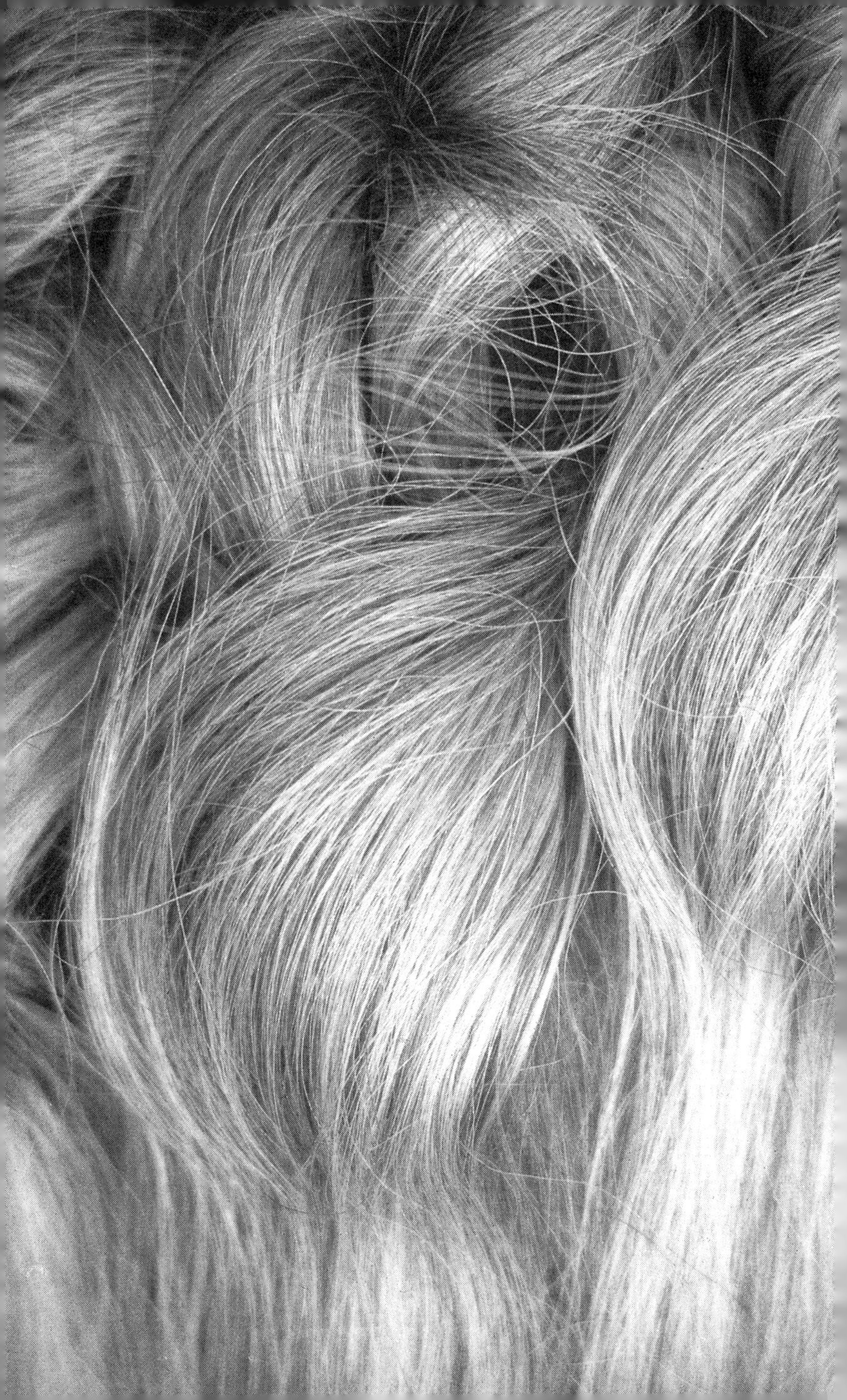

image behind the lens. The reproduction scale is therefore a most important criterion in the design for a lens and for its optical corrections. These two factors are defined for a reproduction scale of 1:8 as the limit value. Reproduction scales in excess to this value are considered general photography; values below this are considered as close-up photography. Slight deviations in either direction do not affect the basic principle.

Despite complicated computer programs for calculating optical systems, despite new glasses with exceptional characteristics, it is possible to design optical systems with the best possible reproduction characteristics only for a certain focusing range, especially if the lens needs to be reasonably fast. Most lenses are designed for photographing at infinity – they are corrected for infinity. Depending on type of lens and focal length the best shooting distances start at 25 to 100 times the focal length of the lens. The length of the helical focusing movement determines the close-up limit. Using a lens developed for high reproduction quality at infinity for close-up work by the use of intermediate rings will result in some deterioration of reproduction quality. This will become more noticeable the closer we try to get to the 1:1 reproduction scale. Not even a small aperture will be able to counterbalance this deterioration in quality completely. Those who are looking for high reproduction quality in the close-up and macro range will not be satisfied with compromise, but will buy a lens that is designed for the job. The choice is between the newly-designed Pentax AF 100mm,f/2.8 Macro lens or the AF 50mm,f/2.8 Macro lens that is expected to be available soon. Then there are all the macro lenses from the range of Pentax A-lenses without automatic focusing facility. Another choice is the macro head for the Pentax bellows 100mm,f/4 which allows continuous adjustment from infinity down to a reproduction scale of 1:1, manually, of course. The additional use of intermediate rings brings the reproduction scale beyond the 1:1 boundary, i.e. the subject is represented at an enlarged scale on film. But this is the equipment that will be used by the professional macro photographer, for the occasional close-up photography there are other, less expensive solutions.

However, if you decide to go beyond the ordinary bounds of close-up photography, I would not recommend a number of intermediate rings between the bellows and the macro head. This would not be very stable, introducing vibrations that make focusing and shake-free shots impossible. From a magnification ratio of about 15:1 the limit of single-step macro photography is reached.

A Zoom is not a macro lens

How does the popular "Zoom with Macro" fit into my description of macro photography? When designers discovered that an additional movement of a group of elements in the zoom lens would take it beyond the close-up limit of 0.8 to 2.0m (reproduction scale 1:10), that was the sensible and practical limit for various focal length zooms. This facility was offered as "macro setting" – reproduction scales 1:4 to 1:7! Sharpness, best possible resolution to the frame edge, contrast and freedom from distortion, were secondary. The description "Macro close-up facility" adopted recently is more realistic. Even so, a zoom lens is by definition designed for variation in focal lengths and is not ideal for close-up photography. Therefore you should not expect too much of this facility. It will be very useful to depict the butterfly on a bloom in your garden, especially if you stop down to f/11 and the falling-off in sharpness towards the edge of the picture helps to enhance the effect of the close-up subject. But if you wish to render a pin-sharp reproduction of a fine ink drawing, then the Pentax AF 100mm,f/2.8 Macro lens is a better tool as it is specifically designed for this type of subject.

From this description of the reproduction characteristics of these lenses we can state a ranking order of suitable equipment for the Pentax SFX. The first place must be reserved for the AF 100mm,f/2.8 Macro lens as it combines excellent reproduction qualities with automatic focusing over the whole range from infinity to a reproduction scale of 1:1. The second place should be occupied by the 50mm,f/2.8 Macro, to be available shortly. Then there are the specialist macro lenses from the Pentax A-system lens range where you will also find 50mm and 100mm macro lenses. Amongst these I would say that the 100mm,f/4 Macro head should rank highest. After that follow the SMC close-up lenses. These supplementary lenses in front of the 50mm standard lens have a slightly degrading effect on the reproduction quality of the prime lens and the variations in reproduction scale are not very big. The Pentax K intermediate rings are more effective in this respect, but the thicker the intermediate ring, the more are the capabilities of the lens stretched and the more deterioration in reproduction quality that has to be accepted.

Universally Useful: The Pentax AF 100mm,f/2.8 Macro Lens and 50mm, f/2.8 Macro Lens

Only lenses that are specifically designed for close-up photography with reproduction scales of 1:10 to 1:1 will meet the requirement of perfect quality. In the Pentax range the choice is between the AF 50mm,f/2.8 macro and the AF 100mm,f/2.8 macro. Both lenses distinguish themselves by excellent reproduction qualities in the close range and both can be focused automatically from infinity to a reproduction scale of 1:1. The structural characteristics of these lenses are different but both are equipped with optical refinements for uniformly high reproduction quality throughout the entire focusing range.

The AF 50mm,f/2.8 macro uses floating elements. This means that not the entire optical system is moved during focusing; an additional group of elements is moved within the system but the rest of the elements remain fixed. In the 100mm macro a 6-element gaussian group moves in front of a fixed 3-element correction group.

Although the AF 50mm, f/2.8 macro is clearly larger and heavier than the AF 50mm, f/1.4 standard lens it could be used as a standard lens with all its typical reproduction characteristics so it is worth considering as an alternative, but the standard lens is much faster than the macro lens. The distance from the front of this macro lens to the subject plane at a reproduction scale of 1:1 is 5cm.
The AF 100mm, f/2.8 macro is a gem and ideal for most applications for which a moderate telephoto lens is generally suited. It is not only a specialist for macro photography but will produce excellent pictures of almost any subject at distances from infinity down to a reproduction scale of 1:1. A further advantage is that the distance from the front of the lens to the focusing plane at a reproduction scale of 1:1 is now increased to 11cm. This is a very important point when shooting small creatures, as one does not have to move quite so close and it is also easier to arrange proper illumination of the subject. Furthermore, the narrower angle of view produces a more pleasant perspective at the greater distance for close-ups and keeps unwanted objects out of the frame.

The two macro lenses with their smooth, sleek exterior lie comfortably in your hand and seem to invite you to hand-held close-up photography. Automatic focusing down to the 1:1 reproduction scale and automatic exposure programs make macro photography easy and pleasurable. The only point that remains to be checked is that the shutter speed displayed in the viewfinder is never slower than 1/125 sec. with either one of these macro lenses. However, if circumstances demand, you could always try a shot at 1/60 sec. if you can support your arm and the camera.

SINGLE or SERVO for close-up subjects?

Once you are familiar with the characteristics of both of these modes then they are both equally suited to produce sharp close-up shots. The choice of the focusing type is mainly determined by the subject. To shoot stationary or sluggish subjects the SINGLE focusing mode is safe. You arrange the subject in the viewfinder with roughly focused lens, then you press the release button lightly to activate the focusing and press fully down to make the exposure. The only thing you have to watch carefully is that the important subject detail is at the centre of the viewfinder. Should you wish to re-align the frame with the main subject off-centre, then you press the release only half-way, allow the autofocus to function, re-align the camera, taking care not to change the distance to the subject, and then depress fully to take the shot. This may sound complicated but is, in fact, one continuous movement, after a little practice!

By setting the camera to SERVO the autofocus computer will continuously adjust the focus to follow the moving subject on its path. The only thing you have to do is keep it in the metering frame at the centre of the viewfinder and depress the release as soon as the green hexagon at the bottom of the viewfinder tells you it is in sharp focus. This is much more difficult if the subject moves at any speed. Despite the excellent technical assistance, you may sometimes be the loser in this race because the subject was one step ahead and as the release may be activated in SERVO even if the subject is not in perfect focus, the shot would have been taken. A better method for checking that the subject is in focus without having to constantly watch the green indicator is to push the main switch to the top position. Now the audible warning will indicate when perfect focus is achieved and your eye can fully concentrate on the subject at the centre of the screen. Corrections with respect to re-aligning the subject area are not possible in SERVO because as soon as you lose the subject from the AF metering frame the autofocus will re-focus on the tree behind and the subject will be out of focus.

Stage switch

The Pentax SF 100mm,f/2.8 Macro lens changes in less than

one second from full-scale landscape photography to a 1:3 reproduction scale picture of the snail on the fence post. It is strange, though it used to take many seconds to adjust a macro lens through its focusing range from infinity to the 1:1 macro scale, I never found it a problem. But the seven-tenths of a second I have to wait now seems much longer. This is the time it takes the AF 100mm macro to move its elements from one shooting range to the other. The Asahi designers must have taken human weakness into account and installed the stage switch on the mount of the AF 100m,f/2.8 Macro lens. If this switch stands across the tube, then the focusing range of the lens is divided into the general far range and the close-up range of 31 to 57cm with a reproduction scale of 1:1 to 1:4. The entire focusing distance is traversed by the autofocus motor in 0.6 sec – fast enough for the impatient to be satisfied. The division of the AF working range at a reproduction scale of 1:4 serves also to indicate that this is the limit for hand-held shooting. This is due partly because it will be necessary to use rather slow shutter speeds to compensate for the smaller apertures needed to obtain a reasonable depth of field. To counteract slight movement in the wind of an outdoor still-life you could place a screen against the wind. To avoid too slow shutter speeds a flash pointed at the subject from above could be the answer.

Manual focusing with the focusing rack

If you decide to focus visually on the focusing screen because the view does not place the main subject at the centre of the screen, then you will disregard the focusing indicator and the audible warning. Both of these aids react only to the part of the subject within the AF metering field. But the very bright and clear image on the focusing screen leaves you in no doubt as to whether the subject is correctly focused, even for extreme macro shots. To achieve fast and accurate focusing you can adopt the following procedure:

Secure the Pentax 30076 focusing rack – or a similar device from another manufacturer – on a tripod and then fix the camera to the rack. Set the AF 100mm,f/2.8 Macro lens manually to the required reproduction scale. To do this you consult the third scale in the distance scale window. Then you move the camera on the rack and check the focus in the viewfinder until the required subject plane is sharp. This method, properly applied, will guarantee technically perfect pictures. This manipulation of the focus will soon demonstrate that from reproduction scale 1:3 it is much easier and more certain to focus by moving the camera rather than trying to focus the lens on the correct distance. The Pentax focusing rack has a 6cm movement to allow for such adjustments.

Even if you use the autofocus of the SFX to find the correct focus which it achieves in fractions of a second, you may afterwards move the camera with lightly pressed release, even if it is on a tripod, to arrange the subject more favourably in the viewfinder. By doing so you would also move the focusing plane that the autofocus had previously determined. For reproduction scales of 1:4 and more, even the slightest movement cannot be fully accommodated by depth of field and the shot will be spoilt. The focusing rack, on the other hand, is an efficient and rigid arrangement and helps to get exact adjustment and alignment of the subject in the viewfinder. Patience in moving the tripod and in arranging the set-up will save you a lot of frustration.

Macro photography in program mode?

Why not? The program mode covers all shooting requirements that the TTL exposure metering is programmed for. This means it can take full account of the loss in lens speed because of the long lens extension necessary for the large reproduction scales. This is due to the fact that the distance of the lens is one-and-a-half times further from the film plane for a reproduction scale of 1:2 than when photographing at infinity. With a reproduction scale of 1:1 it is even twice as far from the film plane. This in turn means that the film gets only half as much light at a reproduction scale of 1:2 and a quarter at 1:1, compared with the lens setting at infinity. The exposure control in the SFX compensates for this loss in speed by setting a slower shutter speed or a larger aperture.

If you use the program mode for close-up shooting then you have to accept the shutter speed/aperture combination that is displayed in the CENTIC panel. If the AF 100mm,f/2.8 lens is in use then the camera will choose the standard program. If we consider the situation of average afternoon lighting, a medium speed film and allowing for the longer lens extension, the exposure electronics will probably calculate EV13. This value is equivalent to f/5.6 and a shutter speed of 1/250 second in the program mode. However, f/8 may be better to allow sufficient depth of field for the subject in hand. You know from your own experience that you are able to hand-hold a shutter speed of 1/125 second, but this combination is not possible either in the fast shutter speed program or in the program for depth of field. The program mode is a quite useful, but not always the ideal shooting mode to use with a close-up subject. Generally you will have to decide between a sufficiently fast shutter speed or a small enough aperture for depth of field. To choose both values ideally is possible only under very good light or with flash illumination.

For the hand-held shot of an unusual subject the main concern is the shutter speed. This must be no slower than your own personal limit. A calm approach and a steadier hand than usual may be worth one whole shutter speed step. Last spring I was able to produce pin-sharp pictures at my own critical shutter speed of 1/125 second with the AF 100mm,f/2.8 Macro lens using a reproduction scale of 1:4. Shots taken at 1/60 second are clearly very risky; either they are sharp, or they are not. Your own experiences will be invaluable in the decision regarding shutter speed against aperture priority. Even a slightly overcast sky with the sun just visible and an average speed film will generally allow you a relatively small aperture and a safe shutter speed. But do not forget to check the shutter speed in the viewfinder when arranging the subject. If you chose aperture priority then you have control of the depth of field, but the shutter speed will have to be watched. If the sun in the afternoon declines to a more interesting angle, but reduces in intensity, then I would definitely switch over to shutter speed priority to preselect my own safe shutter speed. The aperture will have to be chosen with what is left of the available exposure value. This means, of course, that I often work with rather wide apertures, but this does not matter as the AF 100mm,f/2.8 Macro lens possesses excellent reproduction qualities and the focusing screen allows perfect focusing, either manually, electronically assisted or fully automatic. This type of close-up photography will naturally involve only a very small depth of field, which is the penalty for not carrying a tripod. On the other hand one can make a virtue of necessity and present many subjects more attractively in this way. How you should treat a subject is a matter of experience and personal taste. Photography speaks for itself through the pictures. If the subject is in sharp focus, set against either an unsharp background or not, is a matter of personal decision.

Depth of field in a macro picture

How large, or rather how small is the depth of field in close-ups can be seen from the table. At the close range the depth of field is dependent only on the aperture value and the reproduction scale, and not on the focal length of the lens. Therefore the values in the table also apply to the AF 50mm,f/2.8 Macro lens that will be available shortly, and also to the close-up setting on the Pentax AF Zooms, whenever reproduction scales up to 1:4 are possible. The reproduction scale is also the determining factor for the macro setting on zoom lenses.

The old Takumar-Fisheye lens on the modern SFX! All you need is the Pentax K-Adapter. Automatic focusing is not possible, of course, but the working aperture priority mode is no argument for not using this combination.
Photo: Richard Hünecke

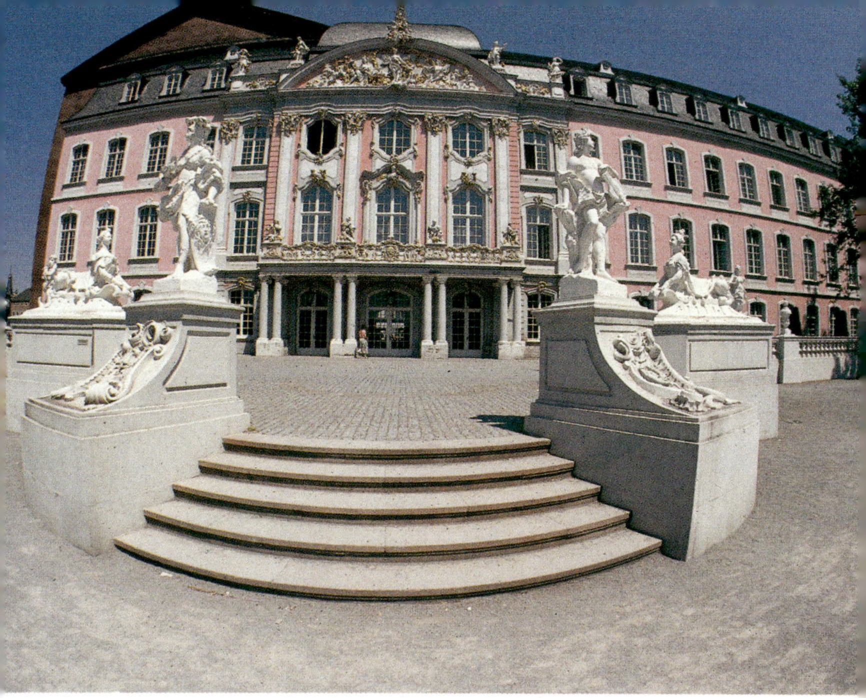

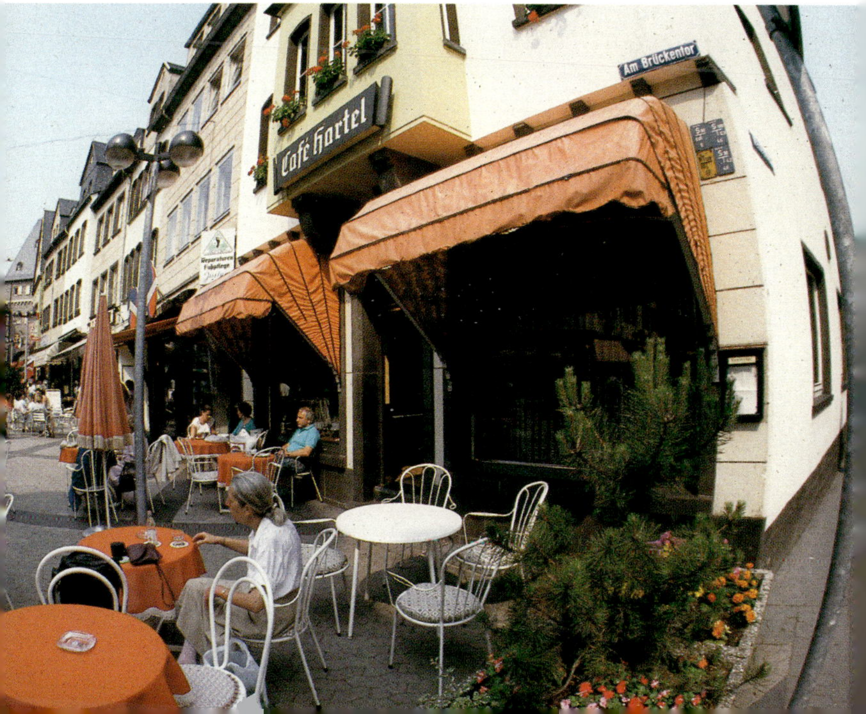

Am Brückentor
Café Hartel

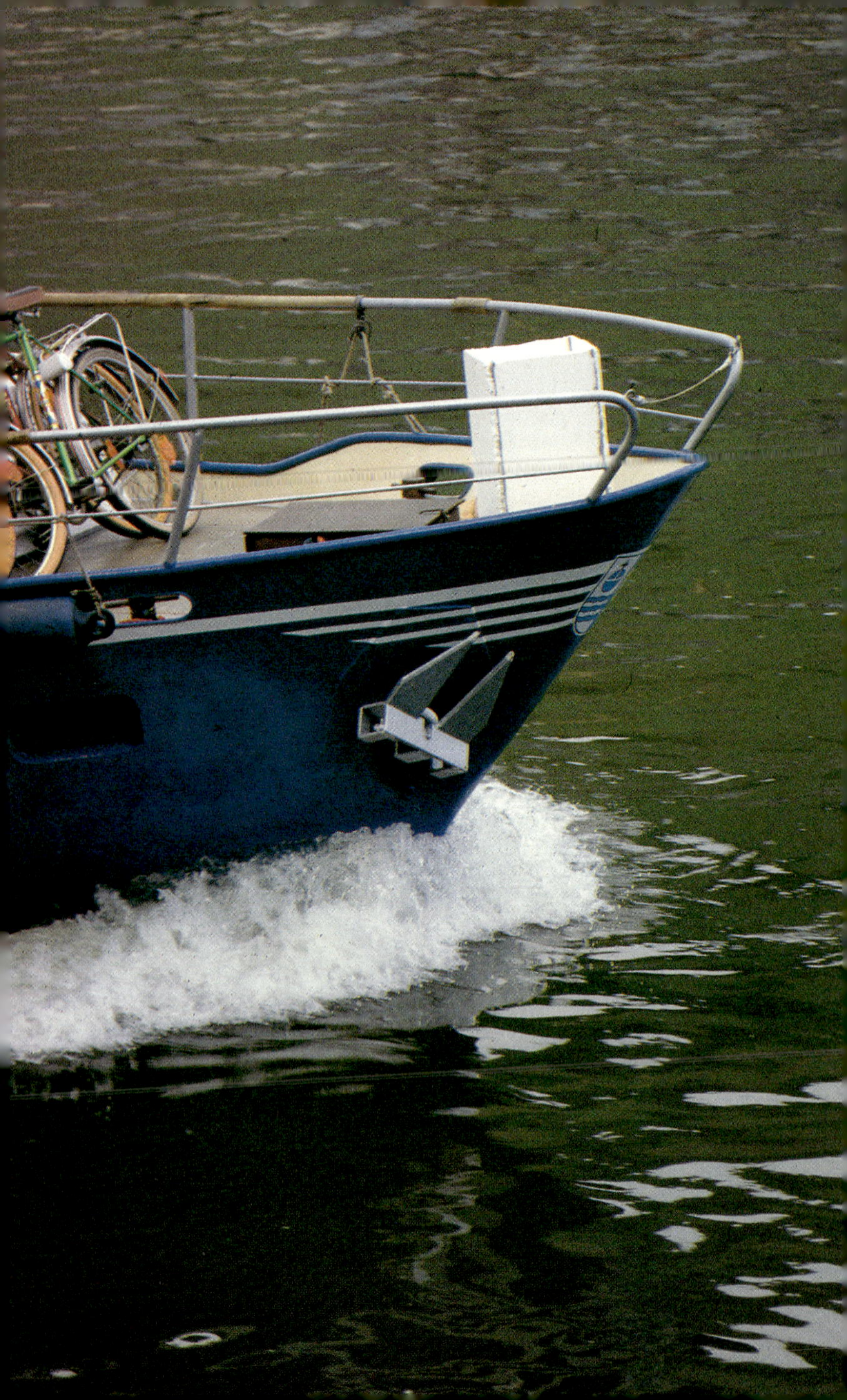

Repro-duction scale	Distance (cm) lens-film plane for focal length			Depth of field (mm) for aperture value							
	50	100	210	2,8	4	5,6	8	11	16	22	32
1:10	60,5	121	254	21	29	41	58	80	117	160	235
1:7,5	49	98	205	12	17	23	34	46	68	92	135
1:5	36	72	151	5	8	11	17	21	33	42	66
1:4	30	62	126	4	6	8	11	15	21	30	•42
1:3	27	53	—	3	4	5	7	9	13	18	26
1:2	22,5	45		1,5	2	3	3,5	6	7	12	14
1:1,5	20,6	41		1	1,3	1,7	2,5	3	5	6	10
1:1	20,0	40		0,3	0,5	0,75	1	1,5	2	3	4
1,5:1	21,1	41,7		0,2	0,3	0,4	0,6	0,8	1,2	1,6	2,4
2:1	22,5	45		0,15	0,2	0,3	0,4	0,6	0,8	1,2	1,6

The values in this table have been rounded up or down. The blurring factor of 0.033mm was taken as the basis for the above values. The depth of field in the close-up zone extends more or less equally in front of and behind the focusing plane.

Why does the table not state any values beyond the reproduction scale 1:1, in particular as the two Pentax AF Macro lenses end at this point? Because both lenses can be taken to a greater distance by intermediate rings K50 and K100. However, only visual manual focusing will be possible, and only the aperture priority program and metered manual modes will be possible from the available shooting modes. These restrictions will have little effect in practice, however. Focusing is now best effected by moving the SFX on the focusing rack 30076 to bring the very narrow zone of sharpness and the focusing plane into agreement.

A further factor is introduced into our attempts to achieve maximum depth of field with the smallest possible aperture: the wave nature of light, which so far has been totally

Even if the motor yacht steers a zig-zag course, the AF SERVO mode guarantees you pin-sharp focus if you follow the bow as it ploughs its way through the water. *Photo: Richard Hünecke*

disregarded. According to optical laws, at a reproduction scale of 1:1, an aperture value of f/22 engraved on the aperture ring becomes f/44, aperture value f/32 becomes in effect f/64. For reproduction scales 2:1 the effective aperture values are now f/66 and f/96! The diffracted rays issuing from these very small apertures have now a much greater effect than at larger apertures. The diffracted rays land adjacent to the points calculated by the optical designers – the depth of field gained by stopping down to apertures f/22 or f/32 is now superimposed with unsharpness due to diffraction. The compromise between gain in depth of field and diffraction unsharpness is called "beneficial aperture". There are tables available which state these values, but if you are like me, you can never find them when you need them. If you adhere to the following three pairs of values you should obtain good results: for a reproduction scale of 1:2 you can stop down to aperture f/22, for a reproduction scale of 1:1 use f/16 and for 2:1 an aperture of f/11 should give you the best results. Under some circumstances you could stop down one more stop, but the sharpness will suffer slightly. Anyway, if you consult your table, the extra depth of field gained is hardly worth it – however, just one millimetre can make all the difference.

AF Zoom for Close-up Photography?

The focal length ring on the Pentax AF Zooms 28-80mm, 35-70mm and 35-135mm, always have "Macro Position" marked beyond the longest focal length. This setting gives a reproduction scale of up to 1:4 which corresponds to a full-frame image of a 15x10cm object. A little searching in a drawer will give you a wealth of suitable objects, and the world is full of objects that make interesting subjects for macro photography. It goes without saying that the autofocus systems of these three AF Zooms also work perfectly at the macro setting. The AF 70-210mm,f/4-5.6 Zoom attains a minimum focusing distance of 1.1m for all focal lengths. At the 70mm setting this means a reproduction scale of 1:12 and at 210mm is it 1:4 – and focused automatically!

With the aperture stopped down by two stops the resulting quality at the macro setting is quite acceptable. However, you should not expect the results to be pin-sharp right to the picture edge. The reproduction of a fine pen drawing will not be as sharp as with a special macro lens. The basic details described for the AF 100mm,f/2.8 Macro lens also apply to macro photography with an AF zoom. For a focal length of 210mm the shutter speed should not be slower than $^{1}/_{250}$ second for hand-held shots. As far as exposure programs are concerned you can use them all at the macro setting with the AF Zoom, but be very careful to watch the shutter speed, put your SFX on a tripod, or use flash.

Close-up Photography with Older Pentax Lenses

Using K-/KA- close-up equipment will only interest the photographer who wishes to use his existing Pentax equipment. If you have just started to use the Pentax system by buying the SFX, then you will be well-equipped with the AF 100mm,f/2.8 Macro lens.

The best lenses from the A-system are the SMC-A 100mm,f/2.8 Macro and the SMC-A 50mm,f/2.8 Macro. Both give a reproduction scale down to 1:1 and can be combined with all the exposure programs available on the SFX. In practice, the only difference between these two lenses and the AF 100mm Macro is that they have to be focused manually. The focus is checked either visually on the focusing screen or by the LED arrows below the viewfinder image. Again, don't forget that the important subject detail has to be positioned within the AF metering area at the centre of the viewfinder.

The most useful trick for close-up photography with KA- and K-Macro lenses is the "snap-in-focus" method. To do this, set the SFX to SINGLE, set the macro lens to the required reproduction scale, push the release all the way down and slowly move the camera towards the subject, always keeping the important subject detail in the AF metering field. When the red arrow vanishes and the green indicator lights up to show that sharp focus has been achieved, release the shutter. This method will guarantee you a sharp picture at all times; it is a pity that it does not work with AF lenses!

If the reproduction scale of the macro lens is insufficient for your purposes, then you can put one or more Pentax automatic intermediate rings between the camera and the lens. These do not possess all the necessary contacts so only the aperture priority and the metered manual modes will be possible, or else manual focusing with sharpness control on the focusing screen, aided by the LED indicators, or the "snap in focus" method.

The SMC-A 100mm,f/4 Macro lens has similar specifications to the SMC-A 100mm,f/2.8 Macro, with the difference that it is not so as fast and its focusing movement brings the reproduction scale to only 1:2.

The next interesting item from the existing Pentax range is the bellows. Its extension of 38mm to 170mm allows uniform setting from infinity down to a reproduction scale of 1:1 with the Macro head SMC 100mm,f/4 Pentax Bellows. Because the preset aperture value on the lens cannot be transmitted by the bellows to the SFX, and the diaphragm control is not transmitted to the lens, you will need a release cable for the SFX and also a wire release to the lens carrier of the bellows. Using the two-thumb synchronization you first close the lens aperture by the wire release and then you operate the SFX by the release cable. This method is also used if the lens attached to the bellows is an AF lens. The SFX is set to aperture priority; it will react correctly to the manually stopped down aperture.

On re-assessing the combination of bellows with the Macro head 100mm,f/4, one has to come to the conclusion that the same setting range and reproduction ratios could be achieved with a great deal more ease in handling, greater certainty, and much more speed by using the Pentax AF or Pentax A 100mm,f/2.8 Macro lens directly on the SFX. The bellows is a tool for the macro specialist for the 2x to 15x magnification of the subject. Even then, the best possible reproduction will require the use of micro lenses with focal lengths of between 12.5mm and 50mm, which are available from Canon, Leitz and Zeiss. These are fitted with microscope thread W 0.8x$^{1}/_{36}$in. To attach the micro lens to the Pentax bellows you proceed as follows: first you screw it into the Novoflex connection ring LEIMIK, which at its rear has Leica thread M39x1 for transition ring M39/T2, and which in turn is screwed into the T2 adapter with Pentax bayonet. Micro lenses have only a simple manually operated iris diaphragm. Focusing is done by moving the bellows after the required magnification scale has been set by appropriately long bellows extension. The correct position of the focusing plane for the fraction of a millimetre-wide depth of field is controlled by visual inspection on the focusing screen of the SFX. The electronic focusing aid by LED indicators and the "snap-in-focus" method also works with the bellows, but its actual usefulness in micro photography depends mainly on the structure of the subject. You will have to try out all the available possibilities for yourself. The SFX is best set to aperture priority mode or metered manual mode, and the aperture is stopped down by at most four stops because of diffraction blur.

The SMC close-up lenses

A close-up lens can be screwed into the filter thread of an AF lens to reduce its focal length. This in turn results in smaller distances to the subject and larger images of the subject on film. The only combination of interest with the AF lenses is with the close-up lenses S25 and S40 which are designed for use with the standard lens. The AF 100mm,f/2.8 Macro lens needs no close-up lens; for the AF 300mm,f/4.5 ED/IF there is none available; and the AF Zoom does not accommodate close-up lenses in its filter thread. Close-up lenses S40 and

S25 – the "S" denotes standard, the number denotes focal length in cm – are available for filter threads E49 and E52.

With close-up lens S40 the standard AF lenses 50mm,f/1.4 and 50mm,f/1.7 give a reproduction scale of 1:3.7. Close-up lens S25 brings the reproduction scale to 1:2.8.

Close-up lenses do not affect the mechanical and electrical connections between AF lens and SFX. Using these lenses is therefore exactly the same as without them as far as exposure programs, focusing, and handling are concerned. If you start your photographic life with the SFX and with just the standard lens then one of these close-up lenses is the easiest and quickest way into macro photography. They also have the additional advantage that there is no loss in lens speed. If you use your exposure programs in such a way that the resulting aperture is down to at least f/8, then you should be very satisfied with your results.

Automatic intermediate rings

These are also suitable for use with the Pentax SFX. As they are connected between the lens and the camera they interrupt some of the communications between camera and KAF- or KA- lenses. Both types of lenses may be used with aperture priority or metered manual modes. The AF lens has to be focused manually, focus control being either by visual inspection on the focusing screen, or by electronic focusing aid by LED indicators. The "snap-in-focus" method will also work.

There are five different automatic intermediate rings available: the set of three rings, 12mm, 19mm, and 26mm in length, form the usual set of interchangeable extensions. The other two: K50 which is 50mm long and K100, 100mm long, are intended for lenses of longer focal lengths. All rings transfer the preset aperture value on the lens for open aperture metering, and from there the diaphragm action back to the lens.

The three smaller intermediate rings bring the AF 50mm standard lens in stages down to a reproduction scale of 1:1.

Both of the larger rings, K50 and K100, achieve a reproduction scale of 1:2.5 with the AF 300mm,f/4.5 ED/IF lens. I also include two examples for combining the SFX with intermediate rings and SMC-A lenses: ring K50 brings SMC-A 85mm,f/1.4 to a reproduction scale of 1:1.4 and SMC-A f/300mm to 1:3.7. Ring K100 takes these two lenses to reproduction scales of 1.2:1 and 1:2.5 respectively, which is clearly much beyond the reproduction scale for which they had been designed. The closer we take a non-macro lens, by whatever means, to a reproduction scale of 1:1 the more its reproduction qualities will suffer. With the aperture stopped down at least three stops to obtain better depth of field, the quality will nevertheless be quite reasonable around the centre of the picture, but will decline more or less rapidly towards the edges. To obtain good reproduction quality right across the frame you will have to opt for a macro lens.

The automatic intermediate rings are quite uncomplicated and relatively inexpensive companions for travel. Frame and reproduction ratio is adjusted by helical gear on the intermediate ring. However, the longer the ring, the less space for movement – you will need at least two rings to obtain sufficient space to be flexible. Once you have tried out the two rings you will soon want to have the third. And once you have counted the cost of these accessories you will come to the conclusion that it may have been better to opt straight away for the AF 100mm f/2.8 Macro that offers more convenience and better reproduction quality.

In the Pentax range of lenses is the SMC-A 200mm,f/4 ED. This lens has no autofocus function, but its particular interest lies in the fact that it can be focused down to a reproduction scale of 1:1. This facility is perfectly complemented by the electronic focus aid and "snap-in-focus". The reproduction scale of 1:1 is possible at a shooting distance of 55mm, and this is a very comfortable distance to bring a wide variety of small subjects onto film at large scale. The only thing that will make you think twice about obtaining this lens is its price!

Sunshine from the Camera

Electronic flash! To make photography independent of daylight, to be able to shoot even if the steadiest hand cannot hold the camera still, you need artificial lighting. A feature of electronic flash is its extremely short illumination time. This is always much shorter than the travelling time of the shutter blind across the film plane (disregarding the longer illumination times of studio flash). The shutter is unable to control flash exposures. It is designed for the continuous illumination from daylight or tungsten lamps. Correct exposure with flash illumination is therefore the duty of the lens. Unlike natural lighting, flash has a rather short range. Furthermore, of course, the intensity of its illumination diminishes as the square of the distance from it. For correct exposure the distance of the flash from the subject determines the aperture. This is expressed in the guide number for the flashgun:

$$\text{guide number} = \text{aperture} \times \text{distance}$$
$$\text{aperture} = \text{guide number} \div \text{distance}$$

where the distance in metres is the distance from the flash source to the subject.

As the aperture is now responsible for controlling the flash exposure it cannot be used solely for controlling depth of field. The flashgun's guide number is an invariable quantity for a given film speed. This means that the size of the aperture is determined by the distance of the flashgun from the subject.

The introduction of computer flashguns has brought a certain freedom of choice of aperture as these have usually two, three or even four adjustable light outputs, for which an appropriate aperture may then be selected. The rest is then done by the computer in the flashgun with silicon photo diode and associated circuitry. It works as follows: the photo diode measures the light reflected by the subject during flash illumination. As soon as the output calculated from the preset

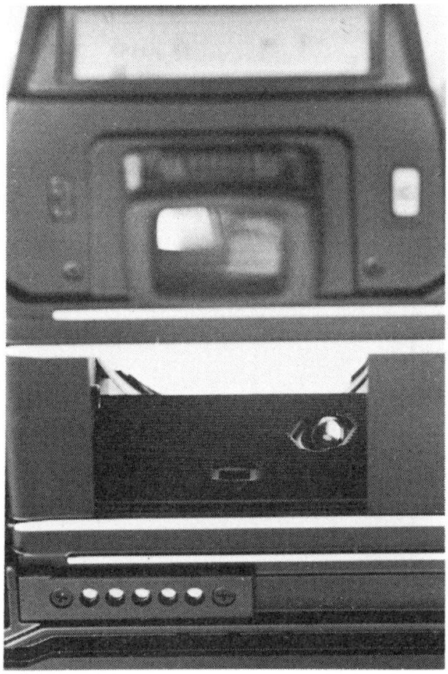

The view through the SFX from the back: on the right is the large eye of the silicon photodiode for TTL flash metering, at the centre is the rectangular window of the AF sensor, and beneath the film guides are the contacts for the data back.

aperture and programmed film speed is reached, the flash computer turns the flash off. Any colour filter or other accessory on the flash reflector, and the flash distance, are automatically taken into account. However, colour filters in front of the lens and increased camera extensions for macro shots have no effect on flash duration and have to be taken into account separately.

TTL flash control, a facility available for some years in Pentax cameras, also allows the lens aperture to be chosen on the basis of depth of field. Put the new Pentax AF 400 FTZ or another flashgun from the AF-T/C series into the hot shoe of the SFX (don't forget where you have put the cover, only the AF 400 FTZ has a safe place for it!), or connect it via the TTL cable to the camera. The flash is set to TTL-AUTO and the

SFX to aperture priority. In the time it takes to decide on depth of field and aperture, the flashgun capacitor will have charged and the shutter on the SFX will have automatically adjusted to the flash synchronization time of $^1/_{100}$ second. The choice of aperture extends over the whole range available on the attached lens. The smallest aperture will give you the largest depth of field from close to the camera to the farthest corner of the room – provided the flash output is sufficient for that range; a wide open aperture will limit your depth of field. Then you release. The first shutter blind will start its journey across the film and pass the trigger impulse to the flashgun – the flash operates. The silicon diode of the SFX registers the light from the subject by the reflection from the film surface. This is compared with the reference value calculated by the camera computer. As soon as the metered impulse reaches this value, the thyristor switches the flash off. The second shutter blind follows to cover the film.

The TTL flash control automatically considers all factors that normally affect flash photography: distance from flash to subject, filter or other accessories in front of the flash reflector, light reflection from the subject, filter in front of the lens, the effective aperture value and, of course, the extra illumination requirement necessitated by any camera extension for macro shots. For TTL flash control it is also quite immaterial whether the flash was pointed directly at the subject or bounced from the ceiling, through a diffuser, against an umbrella, etc. As far as the output of the flash is concerned, the amount of light will be correctly metered by the TTL flash control. The Pentax SFX is capable of all three types of flash control; it only depends on the flashgun which is the most suitable method. All functions available will be subject to one constant factor, the guide number of the flashgun.

The Miniflash under the Cap

We made its acquaintance when we considered the red

metering flash for assisting the autofocus system in distance metering. Now we are talking of the larger side of the reflector that comes to life when the yellow button on the pentaprism is depressed.

The yellow button causes the reflector to pop up and at the same time the flash is connected to the camera circuit. If you have loaded a lithium battery in the handgrip, then after about 3 seconds the red LED next to the eyepiece will indicate that the flash capacitor has been charged. Now the miniflash with its quite remarkable guide number of 14 for ISO 100/21° film is ready for action. It is capable of illuminating an angle of view equivalent to a lens of 35mm focal length. According to Pentax specifications the lithium battery will support about 300 flashes; alternatively, if four alkaline batteries are loaded in the optional larger handgrip, then the capacity would be 240 flashes. I suspect, however, that this output refers to best possible conditions, i.e. absolutely fresh batteries and shooting in the close range with a rather large aperture.

The miniflash can be used together with any of the shooting modes. Should you wish to have full control over depth of field, then you would select aperture priority mode or metered manual mode. In these two modes you are free to use any available aperture. Control of flash output according to film

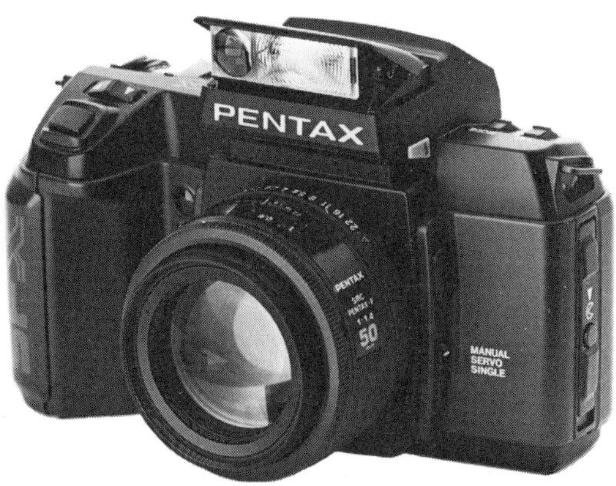

The mini flash pops into action at the push of a button. Its guide number is 14 for ISO 100/21° film and it is controlled by the TTL automatic function.

speed and subject distance is performed automatically by the TTL flash control.

The following table gives the distance range of the flash for different apertures.

Aperture	ISO 100/GN14	ISO 400/GN28
1,4	10 m	20 m
2,0	7 m	14 m
2,8	5 m	10 m
4,0	3,5 m	7 m
5,6	2,5 m	5 m
8,0	1 7 m	3,4 m
11	1,3 m	2,6 m
16	0,9 m	1,8 m
22	0,6 m	1,2 m

If the SFX is set to shutter speed priority or program mode, then the camera's computer will take care of the exposure data. First it will select the flash synchronization speed, $^1/_{100}$ second if the ambient lighting conditions are very good, otherwise $^1/_{60}$ second. Then it will calculate the appropriate aperture, which is usually kept small to retain a little of the atmosphere. If, however, the flash is activated for very sunny subjects, then it will select $^1/_{100}$ second and the appropriate aperture. In this case it will act mainly as a fill-in flash, lightening heavy shadows of a back-lit scene. The actual flash measurement will be performed by the automatic TTL flash control. In the latter two exposure modes you have no control over any of the settings. The automatically-selected shutter speed is displayed in the viewfinder and in the CENTIC display panel – either $^1/_{100}$ second or $^1/_{60}$ second. In the aperture priority and manual exposure modes the selected aperture is also displayed.

Because the AF 100mm,f/2.8 Macro and the AF 300mm,f/4.5 ED/IF extend rather far forward into the projected beam of the flash, they cannot be used with the miniflash. If the camera's electronics detect the presence of either of these two lenses it will inactivate the miniflash. AF Zooms may be used with the miniflash from the 35mm focal length setting.

The Perfect Partner for the SFX: The AF 400 FTZ

The AF 400 FTZ represents the ultimate in power that can be accommodated by a compact flash and mounted in the hot shoe. And why is the hot shoe of the SFX on the right camera shoulder? Because this flashgun, weighing nearly 500g, is quite a weight but is very well balanced in this position. I have held even lighter arrangements which have felt much less stable than this well-designed hand-held equipment. The little hot shoe cover can be safely stored on the special slot in the AF 400 FTZ.

Technical data for the AF 400 FTZ:

- ○ Guide number 40 for ISO 100/21°, together with the AF 400 T the most powerful flashgun in the Pentax range.
- ○ Power supply: 4 alkaline batteries, 1.5V, type AA/LR6 or 4 AA-size NC rechargeable batteries.
- ○ Flash durations: 1/500 to 1/30000 second depending on subject and aperture.
- ○ Power shut-off device: the flashgun automatically switches itself off if the release has not been pressed for more than 3 minutes.
- ○ Recharging times: 0.3 to 9 seconds for absolutely fresh alkaline batteries, 0.3 to 6 seconds for freshly recharged NC batteries.
- ○ Film speed: automatically read into the flash from the SFX.
- ○ Illumination angle: adjustable via zoom reflector for focal lengths 105, 50, 35, 28mm, additional diffuser for 24mm.
- ○ Indirect flash: zoom reflector may be tilted through to 90° upwards, 90° to the left and 180° to the right.

- Special characteristics: integrated and separately controllable red metering flash with 7m range as focusing aid for the SFX autofocus system. Any uncertainty in focusing is indicated in the viewfinder by the two red flashing arrows.
- The flash triggering point can be shifted by slide switch to before the second shutter blind is released.
- The five illumination angles and the two output rates result in the following guide numbers:

Guide Number for ISO 100/21°		
for focal length	with output stage	
mm	1/1	1/16
105	44	11
50	40	10
35	34	8,5
28	29	7,2
24 with diffuser	20	5

The guide numbers for other film speeds may be calculated by multiplying the following table values:

for ISO 25/15°	x 0.5	for ISO 400/27°	x 2.0
for ISO 50/18°	x 0.7	for ISO 800/30°	x 2.8
for ISO 200/24°	x 1.4	for ISO 1600/33°	x 4.0

Rules for the AF 400 FTZ

Actually there are only two: for both you set the flashgun to TTL-AUTO. The actual choice is then made via the MODE switch. The automatic TTL control will adjust the flash output perfectly to the film speed and shooting conditions. Why should you switch the AF 400 FTZ to manual operation if it is

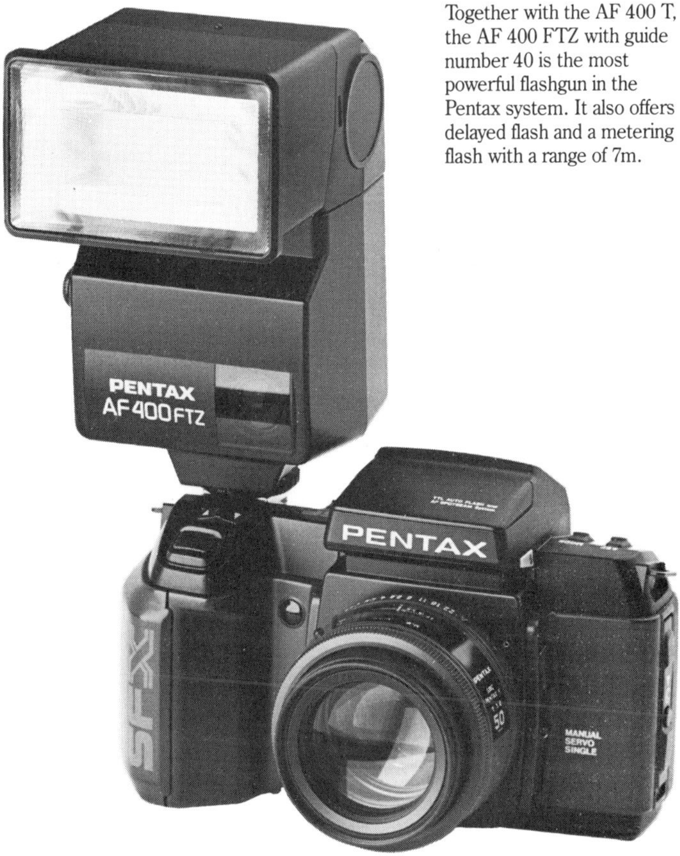

Together with the AF 400 T, the AF 400 FTZ with guide number 40 is the most powerful flashgun in the Pentax system. It also offers delayed flash and a metering flash with a range of 7m.

so easy and safe to use the automatic function? Perhaps for extreme subject conditions. For instance if we want to ensure that we have the best possible chance to show a display of figures on the 30m tower of the town hall, then we would want to use its full power together with a large aperture to catch it on film reasonably well illuminated.

The most straightforward method is as follows: set the SFX to program mode or shutter speed priority and the flash to TTL-AUTO. As soon as the release is slightly pressed the associated electronics of camera and flashgun will set the shutter speed to either $^1/_{60}$ or $^1/_{100}$ second, depending on ambient lighting conditions, and select a rather large aperture in relation to the lighting conditions and film speed. This combination of values will not always give you the desired depth of field, but it will ensure that the background is reasonably well lit. In the automatic mode you are not able to influence any of the settings. If you want to know what aperture the automatic program mode is going to select, you can press the "ML" button and the shutter speed and aperture value will be displayed in the CENTIC panel. In the viewfinder you will see the shutter speed, "P" for program mode and the flash symbol which indicates that the attached flashgun is ready charged. Now it only depends on the subject and if you can frame it in the viewfinder for your desired shot.

Second possibility: here too the AF 400 FTX remains set to TTL-AUTO, the SFX is set to either aperture priority mode or metered manual mode. Now you can select the appropriate aperture for the desired depth of field: either a large aperture for a portrait taken with indirect flash, or a small aperture for a large depth of field to depict the interior of the old valve radio sharply from front to back. When the release is lightly pressed you will only see "M" or "A" and the flash symbol in the viewfinder, in the CENTIC panel only the automatically selected shutter speed of $^1/_{100}$ second. The aperture value you know anyway, because you have selected it on the aperture ring.

Further rule: the focal length value that lights up at the back of the AF 400 FTZ has to correspond to, or be smaller than, the focal length of the attached lens, otherwise the whole frame will not be illuminated. Therefore don't forget to change the position of the zoom reflector when changing the focal length of the lens. The ZOOM slide switch on the rear of the AF 400

Diffuse, reflected, sunlight has its own particular charm. In many situations it would be wrong to upset the soft lighting by using a fill-in flash. AF 24-50mm Zoom. *Photo: Richard Hünecke*

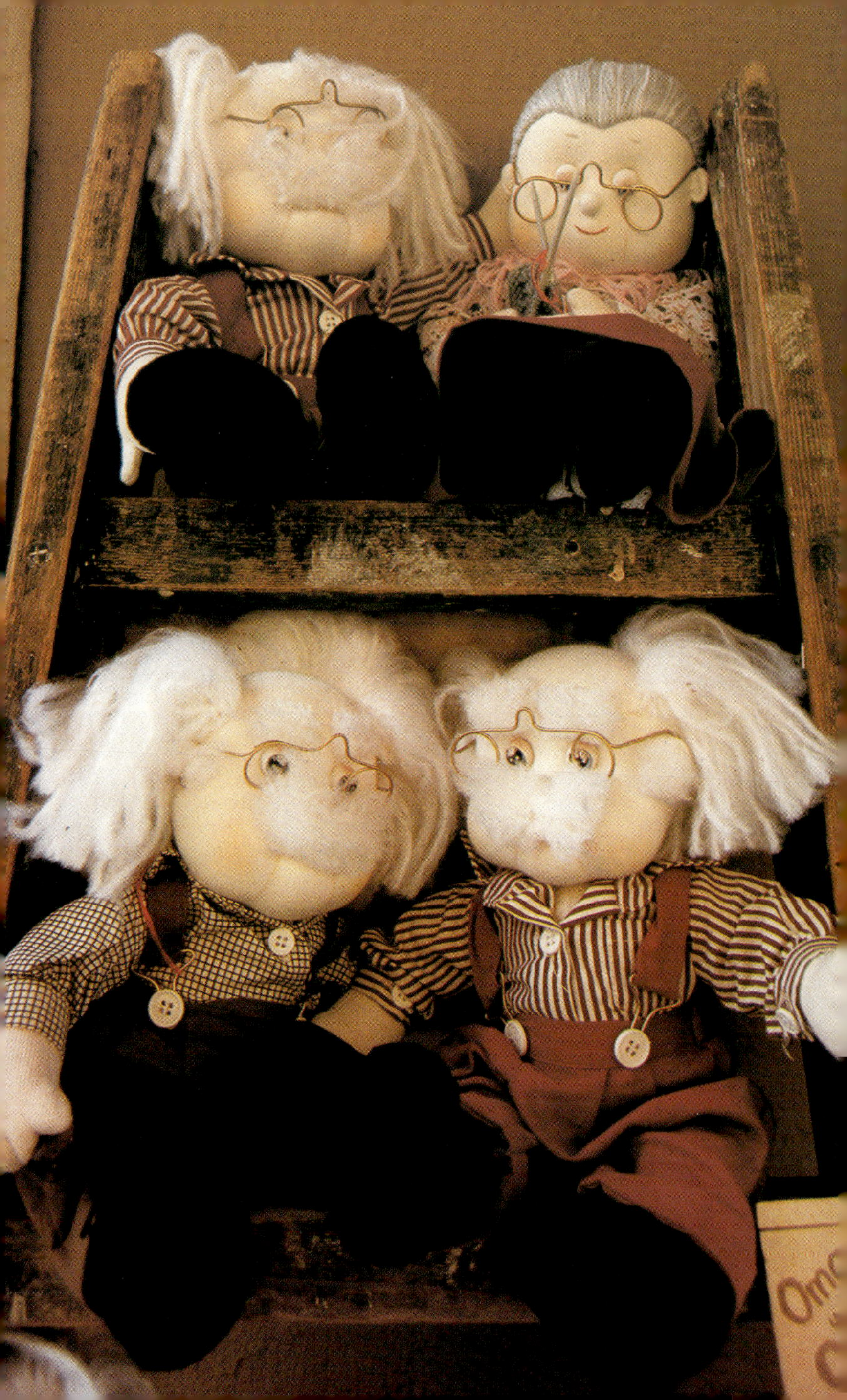

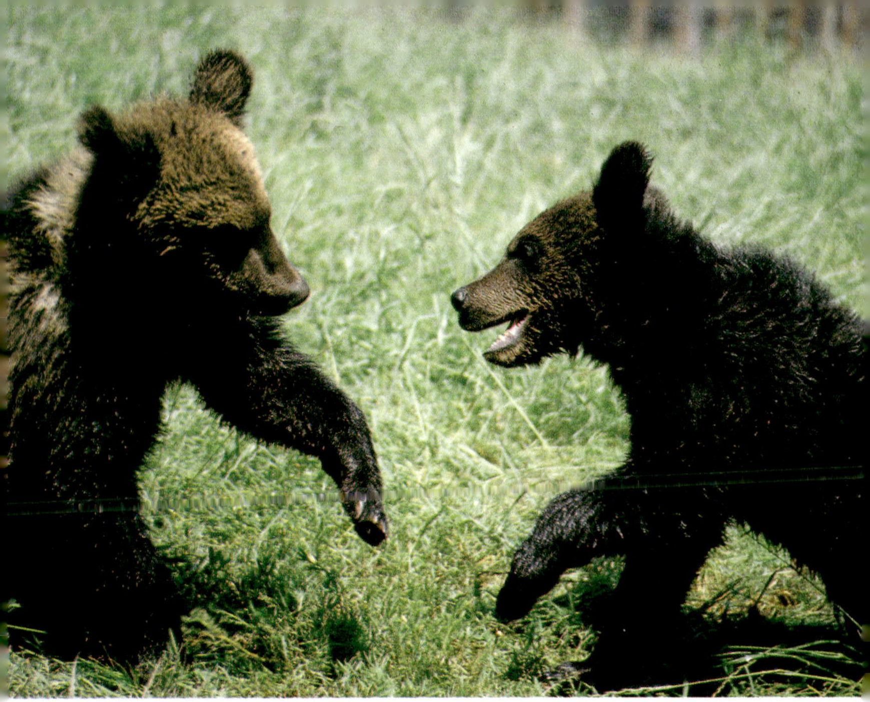

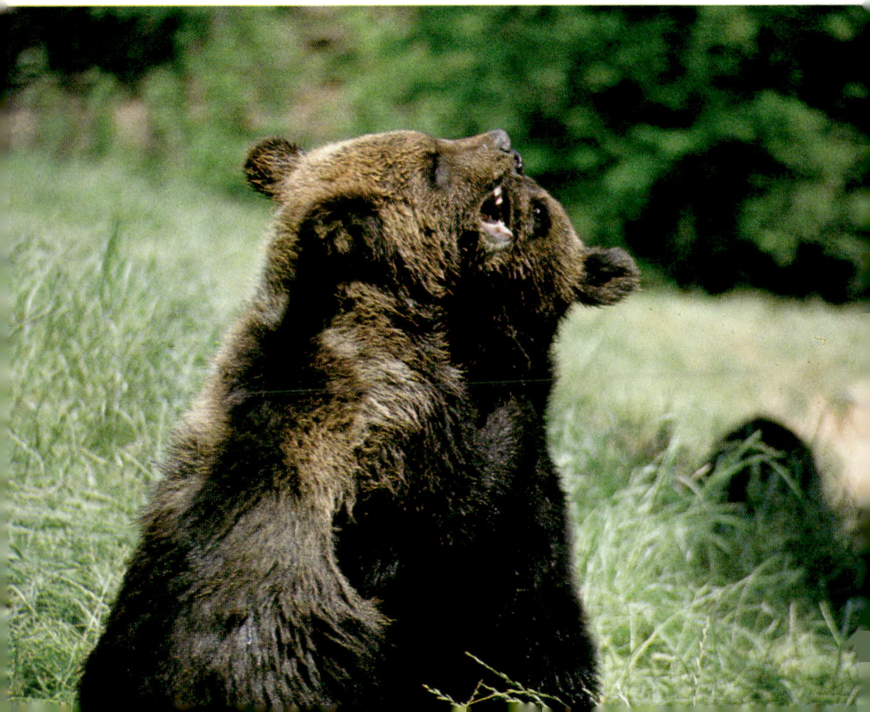

FTZ adjusts the scale in the the calculating table for the appropriate focal lengths.

Changing the flash trigger point

A small switch at the rear of the AF 400 FTZ is used to select the flash trigger point from just after the first blind exposes the whole film area, or a fraction of a second before the second blind is programmed to follow. In this case the shutter is automatically set to 1/60 second, but such a "fast" shutter speed will not give you any interesting effects. You have to change to MAN and select a slower shutter speeds – and use a tripod! If you choose the aperture wisely you will end up with a faint and very effective blurred image of your moving subject up to the point when it is frozen by the flash fired just as the shutter closes. This is more realistic for moving subjects because you catch a sharp image with blurred streaks leading up to it. When the flash is fired in the conventional way as the

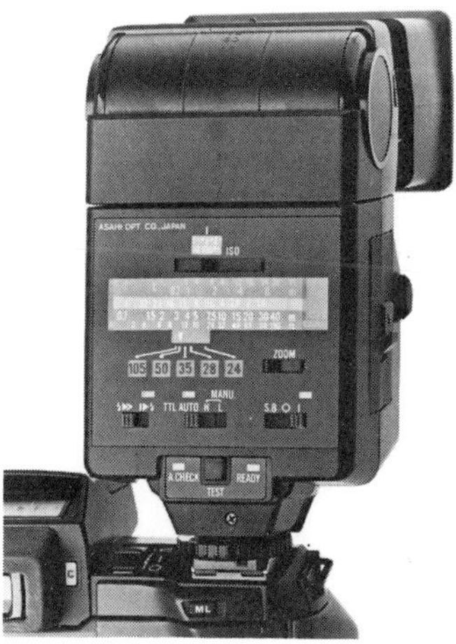

The control centre of the AF 400 FTZ is clear and logically arranged. You know right away what to do – even without the manual.

Young bear cubs playing – a subject one could hardly resist! Shutter speed priority, fast shutter speed, AF Servo and single frame shooting should be the right formula to ensure success. AF 70-210mm Zoom.

Photo: Richard Hünecke

shutter opens, the blurring can happen after the flash, so the subject looks as if it is moving backwards.

Make the Most of your Flash!

Flash fired directly at a subject lights it up properly, but it is not very attractive in many cases. The AF 400 FTZ offers suitable facilities for countering this harsh direct lighting.

First step: turn the zoom reflector upwards to the ceiling or sideways to a white or light-toned wall. There is one disadvantage, even if the ceiling or the wall are brilliantly white, the resulting illumination is not absolutely predictable. If it is possible to calculate the distance that the flash travels to the ceiling and back to the subject then there is still the uncertainty of the reflectivity of the surface. The TTL flash control can cope with this problem. Even so, it could be that the model is illuminated flatly by a rather uninspiring light source instead of with pleasing modelling.

Second step: take the AF 400 FTZ out of the hot shoe of the SFX and connect it via a 5P SyncCord F-cable to the camera. Now you are free to position the flash on the 1m length of cable to illuminate the subject at an angle from the right, left, above or below. The side opposite to the flash will be left in shadow, and sometimes this is rather dark. You have two means at your disposal to fill-in this shadow. Either you position a large white reflecting surface in such a way that some of the light is reflected onto the subject. A screen, white sheet, white plastic board, or similar surface will serve this purpose. To have the right effect the size of the reflecting surface should be about 1x0.8m for a portrait and 2x1.3m for a standing figure; it should also be as close as possible to the model without actually coming into the picture.

Other possibilities of filling in shadows require a little more thought. The AF 400 FTZ cannot be combined with other flashguns and there is no facility for connecting two or three AF 400 FTZ flashguns to the SFX. If more than one flash is the important criterion, but the delayed flash, AF metering flash and zoom reflector are of secondary importance, then you could choose the AF 400 T (guide number 40) or the AF 280 T (guide number 28) for the SFX because these allow the combination with one or two other flashguns for filling-in shadows. In that case you will need a flash distributor and four Synchro Cables B, the 5m long cable to allow sufficient freedom of movement. This ability to position the additional sources allows much greater freedom, and is not only useful for filling in shadows. You can arrange it according to model, idea and subject treatment: striking side-light, dramatic illumination from the top, silhouettes against backlighting and so forth. The possibilities are endless. Whatever arrangement you choose, the TTL flash control will always ensure correct exposure. That you would choose either metered manual mode or aperture priority for free control of depth of field by manual aperture setting goes without saying. To go even further you could use one flash distributor and three flashguns of the AF/T series on 5m long TTL cables. If these three are not enough, then you could combine two distributors and then you would have enough connections for five AF/T flashguns. The individual lengths of the TTL cables should be no more than 5m if you are connecting that many flashguns.

From point source to diffuser

How about setting your favourite model in a spectacular soft lighting situation? Hang a sheet of 1.5m wide translucent paper from ceiling to floor, place the three flashguns behind this screen some distance apart from each other and so that one is higher than the other two. Ask the model to pose in front of it at a distance of about 1.5m. Now you won't need a modelling light to determine the positions of the shadows, only a discreet background light, and a comfortable atmosphere to inspire your model in your studio. The essential trick for soft glowing flash is a large, reflecting surface fairly close to the model. Only if it is placed close enough will stray light be able to filter around the subject to soften the outlines and reduce heavy shadows.

Should your budget not allow any more investment at this moment, go and buy some large insulation boards from a DIY store, about 1x0.5m and glue some household aluminium foil to one side of the board. Two such boards can be used as reflecting surfaces for the AF 400 T or AF 280 T, the other two for filling in shadows. What remains is a matter of proper positioning to place the right amount of light in the right areas. The reflecting surfaces should be fairly close to the subject, but take care that neither the reflectors nor the flashguns themselves send their light beams directly back to the lens. The different reflecting qualities of white board and aluminium foil cannot be described, you have to try them out yourself.

The more expensive route to soft flash illumination is to buy one of the photographic umbrellas which are offered in 80cm and 1m diameter sizes by several makers. Even if you start with this more professional set-up, you will still have to experiment with one or two films until you master the intricate problems of controlled lighting. To be able to assess the effects of your illumination it is best to use slide film, as this shows gradations in lighting much more clearly.

The following Pentax flashguns can be recommended for multiple flash: AF 400 T with guide number 40, AF 280 T with guide number 28 (one never has too much but sometimes too little light!) and ring flash AF 080 C for uniform illumination of close-up subjects. AF 200 T with guide number 20 is another possibility.

Non-Pentax flashguns will work with the Pentax SFX only as computer flashguns without TTL control and in purely manual operation. These may only be attached directly in the hot shoe or by centre contact cable adapter. The flash synchronization time of 1/100 second or longer has to be set manually on the SFX. Non-Pentax flashguns have no access to the electronics of the SFX.

Little Helpers for Special Needs

Other accessories from the earlier Pentax range may be used with the SFX, but others had to be re-designed. The battery holder for four AA size batteries, external power supply, Flash Adapter F for hot shoe, Cable Release F and the viewfinder magnification lens I have already mentioned. These accessories are useful for general photography. For more specialised use there are a few more items:

Interval Data Back F

This is in the form of an interchangeable camera back and its function is to register various data on the film. The data that may be displayed are the following:

1. The date in one of the following forms: day-month-year, month-day-year, year-month-day.
2. The day's date, hour, minute.
3. A six-digit code in three groups of two
4. A code letter and a number counting in ascending order with each frame from 00 to 99.
5. A code letter and a number counting in descending order with each frame from 99 to 00.

The data, which will be exposed onto the negative in the right lower corner of the frame, are selected by the MODE 1 button, and to activate their exposure on film the PRINT button has to be pressed. Both these buttons are on the Data Back. The exposure is automatically controlled by taking into account the programmed film speed of between ISO 25/15° to ISO 1600/33°.

The interval functions turn the SFX into an automatic photographing device that will take pictures independently of the photographer. The following may be programmed:

1. Day and time of first exposure of a series to be taken within the next 30 days.
2. The time interval between the individual shots. Possible

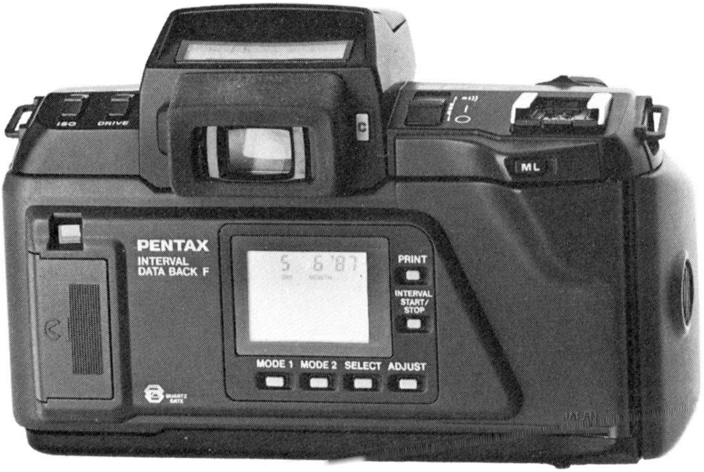

The Interval Data Back F registers and exposes data and identification codes onto the negative and controls the SFX for automatic shooting sequences.

intervals are between 1 second and 99 hours, 59 minutes, 59 seconds.

3. Number of exposures in the series between 1 and 99.
4. Long exposures of 1 second to 99 hours, 59 minutes, 59 seconds.

The data and intervals are entered via the four buttons on the Data Back. What is entered is always displayed on the LCD panel. Once the data has been set the functions are started and stopped by the START/STOP button on the Data Back. The electrical connection to the camera is formed by the five contacts beneath the film guide. The integral clock in the Data Back keeps track of the different lengths of months and leap years and is programmed to run to the year 2085. The quartz clock is precise to +/- 20 seconds per month. Power supply: 2 batteries.

Data Back F

This is the simpler version of the Data Interval Back and is located on the camera in the same way by the two sprung hinges. The contacts in the film guide provide the electronic connection to the camera. Data back F displays the following: 1. The date in one of three forms: day-month-year, month-day-year, year-month-day. 2. The day's date, hour, minute. These data are exposed in the form of 7-segment letters in the right lower corner of the frame when the release is activated. The exposure is again adjusted according to the film speed and is variable between ISO 25/15° and ISO 1600/33°. You can de-activate the exposure of data. The calendar, programmed to the year 2009, will display the current date. The quartz clock is accurate to +/- 90 seconds per month. Power supply 2 silver oxide batteries, 1.5V.

Connection cable for Infra-red Remote Control

This connects the IR receiver which is mounted in the hot shoe of the SFX, with the three-pin remote control socket. The receiver may be turned in its socket through 360°, which allows complete freedom in controlling it from any direction. The transmitter has a range of 60m, but it has to be in a direct, uninterrupted line. Fog will reduce the effective range of the arrangement considerably. An obstacle in the path between sender and receiver, such as a house, a tree, a vehicle, will interrupt the connection altogether. The Pentax infra-red control has three independent channels. It is therefore possible to trigger up to three cameras independently of each other or all three simultaneously. To use this arrangement the Pentax SFX should be set to manual focusing mode because it would automatically adjust its focus if an object moved accidentally into the AF metering area.

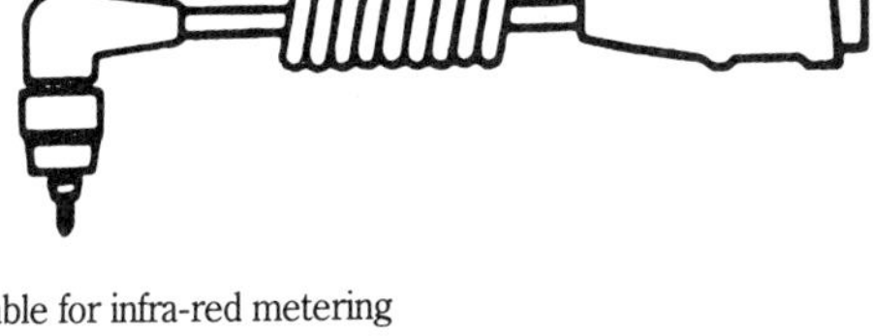

Connection cable for infra-red metering

The Pentax SFX_N

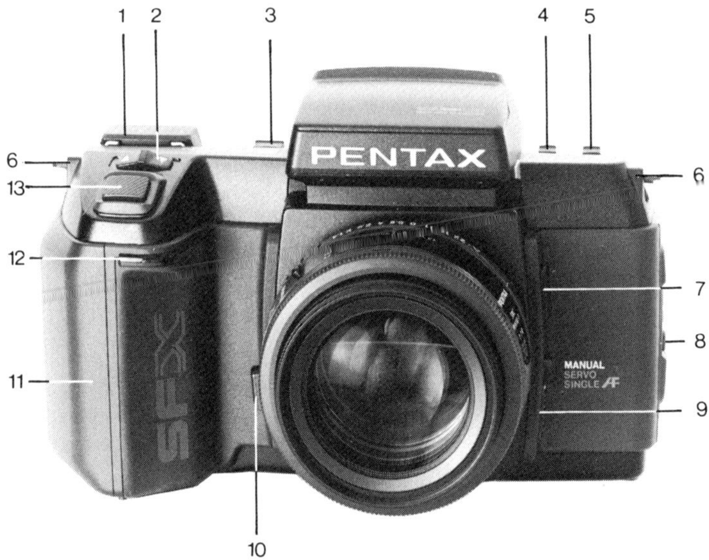

1 Hot shoe with cover
2 Selector switch for input of shutter speed, data, and program selection
3 Main switch
4 Selector switch for exposure programs and film transport
5 Selector switch for film speed and exposure compensation
6 Lug for carrying strap
7 Socket for cable release F
8 Back panel release
9 Autofocus selector switch
10 Lens release button
11 Compartment for lithium battery
12 LED for self-timer
13 Shutter release

Operation of the SFX_N is virtually identical to that of the SFX, except for the additional important facility of automatic exposure bracketing. The SFX_N also has a 1/4000 sec. top shutter speed and a faster flash synch speed of

$1/125$ sec. This latter feature is particularly valuable in reducing the chance of ghost images when using fill-in flash with moving subjects. The viewfinder display of the SFX_N is similar to that of the SFX except, of course, that the top speed is now 4000, but the slowest speed indicated is now 4 ($1/4$ sec.).

The CENTIC panel of the SFX_N can be illuminated when photographing in dim light by pressing the ML button. The camera is supplied with the new standard Lithium Battery Grip FB, but the earlier Lithium Battery Grip and the AA Battery Grip can also be used.

Automatic Exposure Bracketing

There are times when the correct exposure for a particular picture that you have in your mind's eye will not be just a question of proper metering. You may wish to vary the exposure, within certain limits, for particular effects. The colour rendering of slide films, for example, is often better if they are slightly underexposed — the colours appear deeper and more vivid. If you know the precise amount of under- or overexposure you want, you can of course use the DX-override procedure, but you may want to use the professional's technique and take a sequence of exposures, varying the exposure systematically for each one, so that you can select the best result. In this way you will obtain the perfect exposure to suit your view of the picture you want. The Pentax SFX_N can do this for you automatically.

Set the auto-bracketing mode by moving the mode/drive switch towards DRIVE and sliding the select switch in either direction until the [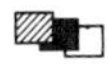] symbol appears in the CENTIC panel. Then set the desired degree of exposure deviation by pressing the +/−EF/ISO switch towards +/− and sliding the select switch. The possible deviation range is from +/− 0.3 to +/− 4.0 in half step increments. The bracketing mode does not work with M, bulb, or 125

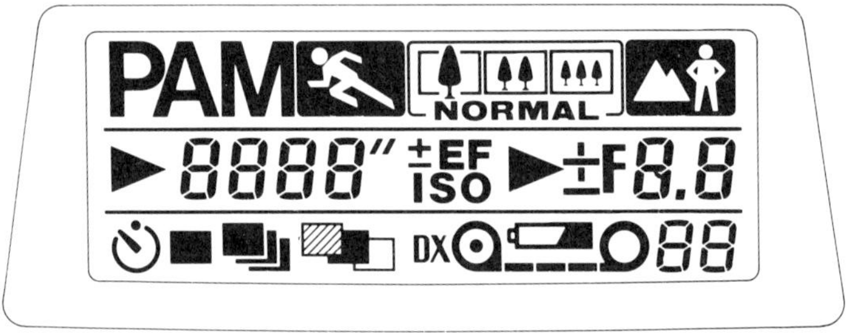

- P — Programmed AE mode
- A — Auto mode
- M — Metered Manual mode
- — Program Action mode
- NORMAL — Normal Program mode
  - Program Tele
  - Program Standards
  - Program Wide
- — Program Depth mode
- ▶ — Priority mark
- 8888" — Shutter-speed/ISO film speed/Bulb mark
- ISO — Manual film-speed setting mark
- ±EF — Exposure compensation mark
- F8.8 — F-number/exposure compensation value
- — Self-timer mark
- — Single frame-advance mode
- — Consecutive film-advance mode
- — Multi-frame self-timer mode
- — Automatic bracketing mode
- — Battery warning
- DX — DX mark/DX override warning
- — Film-loaded mark
- — Film-advance mark
- — End-of-film mark
- 88 — Exposure frame/self-timer counter

settings. The +/−EF symbol in the CENTIC panel blinks to indicate that the bracketing mode is in use.

You may now shoot three frames, either continuously by holding down the shutter release button, or at a chosen interval by pressing the release button for each shot, but in this case don't remove your finger from the release button for more than two seconds or the bracketing sequence will be cancelled. The exposure sequence will be:-

1st frame: +/− 0, or the metered exposure
2nd frame: underexposure by the set value
3rd frame: overexposure by the set value

The viewfinder information will not be displayed for the 2nd and 3rd frames. TTL flash mode is not available with exposure bracketing but the flash will discharge with the first frame if it is switched on.

Multi-frame Self-timer

Besides the normal single-frame self-timer of the SFX described on page 35, the SFX_N can also make multiple exposures with the self-timer. Move the mode/drive switch to DRIVE and slide the select switch in either direction until the [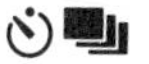] symbol appears in the CENTIC panel. The camera will now take three frames consecutively when the shutter release is pressed. Delays are as follows:-

1st frame: after 12 secs
2nd frame: 2 secs later or after flash recharging time if used
3rd frame: 2 secs later or after flash recharging time if used

The multi-frame mode will cancel automatically after use or if the flash recharging time is more than 7 seconds.

The self-timer indicator lamp on the SFX_N is in the form of a strip above the handgrip.

Lens	Angle of view	Smallest aperture	Elements/ groups	Close-up limit to m	Close-up limit Subject Field cm[1]	Measurements Length mm	Measurements Dia mm	Measurements Weight g	Filter mm	Focusing time s[2]	Remarks
AF 2,8/28 mm	75	22	7/7	0,30	28 × 19	37	64	182	49 E	+	5
AF 1,4/50 mm	47	22	7/6	0,45	24 × 16	37	65	240	49 E	0,5	5
AF 1,7/50 mm	47	22	6/5	0,45	24 × 16	37	65	205	49 E	0,5	5
AF 2,8/135 mm	18	32	8/7	0,70	16 × 11	80	68	400	52 E	+	5
AF 4,5/300 mm ED/IF	8	32	9/7	2,00	21 × 14	160	84	880	67 E	0,8	1, 2, 3, 6
AF 4/600 mm ED/IF	4	32	8/6	5,00	27 × 18	413	181	5800	43 S	+	1, 2, 3, 6, 10, 13
AF 2,8/50 mm Macro	47	32	8/7	0,19	3,6 × 2,4	70	68	385	52 E	+	3,5
AF 2,8/100 mm Macro	24	32	9/8	0,31	3,6 × 2,4	103	74	590	58 E	1,7	3, 4, 6
AF-Zoom 4/24 – 50 mm	84 – 47	22	11/10	0,40	24 × 16	67	69,5	380	58 E	0,3	7, 9
AF-Zoom 3,5 – 4,5/28 – 80 mm	75 – 31	22/32	12/9	0,80 0,40	33 × 22 15 × 10	75	69,5	390	58 E	0,2	7, 9 8
AF-Zoom 3,5 – 4,5/35 – 70 mm	63 – 34	22/32	8/8	0,70 0,32	36 × 24 15 × 10	50	67	250	49 E	0,3	5, 9 8
AF-Zoom 4,0 – 5,6/35 – 105mm	63 – 24	22 – 32	14/12	1,40 0,42	40 × 27 15 × 10	71	72	345	58 E	–	5,9 8
AF-Zoom 3,4 – 4,5/35 – 135 mm	63 – 18	22/32	16/12	1,60 0,75	36 × 24 15 × 10	92	71	485	58 E	0,3	5, 9 8
AF-Zoom 4,0 – 5,6/70 – 210 mm	34 – 12	32/45	13/9	1,10	15 × 10	99	71	555	49 E	0,7	5, 9
AF-Zoom 5,6/250 – 600 mm ED/IF	10 – 4	32	17/15	3,50	19 × 13	435	149	4900	43 S	+	1, 2, 6, 10, 13
AF-Adapter 1,7 ×			6/4			26	64	135		0,3[3]	

Table of Pentax Autofocus Lenses

Notes

1. ED = lens constructed of glasses with extremely low dispersion
2. IF = lens with internal focusing; when focusing on a subject, only one group of elements moves, not the entire optical system
3. Integrated lens hood
4. Lens focusing system in which only the front basic element is moved. The rear groups of correction elements remains fixed for optimum reproduction quality throughout the entire focusing range
5. Use of camera flash is possible with this lens
6. Use of camera flash with this lens is not possible
7. Use of the camera flash is possible from 35mm focal length
8. Reproduction scale and lens field at macro position, which is reached by turning the focal length ring beyond the longest focal length setting
9. Front ring and filter thread turn during focusing
10. Values rounded up or down
11. Focusing time from infinity to close-up
12. Applies for the 5mm long focusing movement of the adapter
13. S = special filter inserted in tube

Index